Move on Maths!
Ages 7–9

The *Move on Maths!* series presents fun, versatile, tried-and-tested maths resources for Years 3, 4, 5 and 6 which you can use in the way that is most suitable for your pupils. The units offer flexible ideas which can be used for maths lessons or homework, and support the Renewed Primary Framework for mathematics. The PNS Framework objectives are clearly shown for every sheet, followed by unit learning outcomes, so it's easy to choose the right worksheet to suit you and your children's needs.

Move on Maths! Ages 7–9

50+ flexible maths activities

John Taylor

Move on Maths! Ages 7–9

50+ flexible maths activities

John Taylor

Routledge
Taylor & Francis Group

LONDON AND NEW YORK

First published 2009
by Routledge
2 Park Square, Milton Park, Abingdon, Oxon OX14 4RN

Simultaneously published in the USA and Canada
by Routledge
270 Madison Avenue, New York, NY 10016

Routledge is an imprint of the Taylor & Francis Group, an informa business

Typeset in Frutiger by
Wearset Ltd, Boldon, Tyne and Wear
Printed and bound in Great Britain by
MPG Books Ltd, Bodmin

British Library Cataloguing in Publication Data
A catalogue record for this book is available from the British Library

Library of Congress Cataloging in Publication Data
Taylor, John, 1953-
    Move on maths! ages 7-9 : 50+ flexible maths activities / John Taylor.
        p. cm.
    1. Mathematics—Study and teaching (Elementary)—Activity programs. I. Title. II. Title: Move on maths! ages seven-nine.
QA135.6.T357 2009
        372.7–dc22   2008031883

ISBN10: 0-415-47153-2 (pbk)
ISBN13: 978-0-415-47153-4 (pbk)

Contents

Understanding Shape

Measuring

Handling Data

Acknowledgements

I would like to thank illustrator Sarah Glenn who has provided drawings for the worksheets. The worksheet exercises were previously printed as part of the Maths Express series published by Ginn.

All 'PNS Framework Objectives' are taken from: *Primary National Strategy: primary Framework for literacy and mathematics* (OPSI, 2006).

Introduction

About this book

Move on Maths! 7–9 Years is a flexible teaching resource, designed to help you with implementation of the renewed Primary Framework for Mathematics in your Year 3 and Year 4 classroom and meet the needs of your students.

The book is complemented by *Move on Maths! 9–11 Years*, a teaching resource for Year 5 and Year 6 that follows the same structure.

Supporting the renewed Framework

This practical workbook provides you with learning material that will enable your students to practise key mathematical principles and practice identified by the Framework. It gives you 26 units for Year 3 and 28 units for Year 4, and these offer you a bank of exercises, examples and activities that can be slotted easily into your lesson planning or given to your students as homework.

The units are organised into four sections, which are designed to broaden and develop understanding of the four key Framework strands:

A   Using and Applying Mathematics
S   Understanding Shape
M   Measuring
D   Handling Data.

Organisation of the book

The user-friendly format of the book makes it easy to find the appropriate unit with support information, activity suggestions and worksheet answers alongside.

Each section is subdivided into resources for Year 3 (ages 7–8) and Year 4 (ages 8–9). The print masters are numbered using the strand letter (A, S, M or D) followed by the year group and the worksheet number. For example, M3/2 is the second Year 3 sheet in the Measuring strand. These numbers are printed as 'thumb tabs' on the right-hand edge of the page.

The Using and Applying Mathematics sections can be used to test if pupils can apply specific skills that have been taught. Worksheets A3/10 to A3/13 and A4/11 to A4/13 link to sheets in the S, M and D sections, as referred to in the teachers' notes.

Unit structure

Each unit is designed around a learning objective from the Framework and contains a **Student photocopiable worksheet** and *Teachers' notes.*

Teachers' notes

These are printed alongside a page of corresponding **Student photocopiable worksheet** and include:

- Learning objective from the Framework
- Notes on prior knowledge and skills that are required
- Suggestions for starter activities and games for group work
- Answers to the worksheet questions.

Whilst the student worksheets are designed to be written on and filled in by your students, the Teachers' notes will support you in introducing the topic, and guide you through prior knowledge your students need to have in order to do the worksheet exercises. They will also give you plenty of ideas for starter activities to get your class stuck into the topic you are asking them to practise in the worksheets.

Student photocopiable worksheets

These practical sheets will give your students plenty of practice in the key mathematical skills and principles. They are designed to accelerate progress through the learning objectives identified in the Teachers' notes.

The sheets provide a wealth of fun exercises, examples and problems for your students to tackle either as part of your main maths lessons, or as their homework. They are written with differentiation in mind: the **challenge sections** that appear in some exercises will support the needs of your more able students.

Their structure is student-friendly and designed to enhance mathematical learning. The worksheets contain the following:

- Quick introduction to the topic that shows the student how to do the exercises
- Drawings to help the students (selected worksheets)
- Questions, exercises and problems to consolidate learning
- Challenge section that contains more difficult exercises and is designed to stretch the more able students.

Unit A3/1 Problems with numbers and number patterns

PNS Framework objectives

- Identify patterns and relationships involving numbers or shapes, and use these to solve problems.
- Derive and recall all addition and subtraction facts for each number to 20, sums and differences of multiples of 10 and number pairs that total 100.
- Derive and recall multiplication facts for the 2, 3, 4, 5, 6 and 10 times-tables and the corresponding division facts; recognise multiples of 2, 5 or 10 up to 1000.

Unit learning outcome

- To solve problems involving numbers and number patterns.

Prior knowledge

- Dividing numbers of objects into two groups – *Are the groups even or is there an 'odd' one?*
- Identifying number sequences – *Are the numbers increasing or decreasing? How much do they change each time?*

Starter activity

- Divide the children into groups of four to six. On the whiteboard prepare a table for results with one column per group. One member of each group collects a double handful of connecting cubes. On the word 'go' each group races to connect the cubes together into two rods. When a group completes this, a member writes in their column of the table how many cubes altogether, plus an 'O' for odd or an 'E' for even at the side. When each group has done this award points on a scoreboard according to the order in which they finished – one for the last, two for second to last, etc.

  One member of each group now collects a second handful to make a second rod. When complete they add it to the table as a second row and again points are awarded for the order of completion. Look at the table and identify groups who had even both times or odd both times. *Have they added an even or an odd number of cubes?*

  Ask groups to join both rods together then divide them in two. Reinforce the point that an even number can be split into two equal halves. *Which groups now have two equal rods?* Award them two bonus points.

Answers to A3/1

1 21   **2** 126   **3** (a)   10   (b) 20   (c) 25 (d) 2   (e) 50   **4** 5
5 (a)   10   (b) 8   (c) 18   **6** 20 red steps, 180 white   **7** (a) Patrick 50; Jak 40   (b) 10
8 36   **9** (a) Becky: 1p, 5p, £1; Hayley: 1p, 10p, 20p, 50p, £2   (b) Becky £1·06; Hayley: £2·82
10 Simon: 10; Richard: 25

Unit A3/1 Problems with numbers and number patterns

1 Sara has six dishes and a bag of sweets. She puts one in the first dish, two in the second, three in the next and so on. How many sweets will she need? ....

2 She starts all over again but this time she puts two sweets in the first dish, double that many in the second, double that into the next and so on. How many sweets will she need now? ....

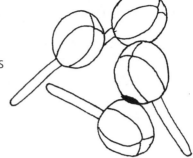

3 Liam has 100 marbles to share equally among some friends. How many will they each get if:

    (a)   he chooses 10 friends? ....

    (b)   he chooses 5 friends? ....

    (c)   he chooses 4 friends? ....

    (d)   he chooses 50 friends? ....

    (e)   he chooses just 2 friends? ....

4 He decides to keep half for himself and shares the rest among ten friends. How many does each friend get? ....

5 Stacey and Chris are delivering papers on opposite sides of the same street. Stacey does the odd-number side and goes to houses 3 to 21. Chris delivers on the even side and goes to numbers 8 to 22.

    (a)   How many papers does Stacey deliver? ....

    (b)   How many papers does Chris deliver? ....

    (c)   How many papers do they need altogether? ....

6 Luke the lighthouse keeper paints the stairs, all 200 of them! He paints every tenth step red and the rest white. How many red steps are there? .... How many white steps are there? ....

7 Two giants run up the stairs. Patrick the giant goes up four steps at a time but Giant Jak can manage five at a time.

    (a)   How many strides does it take each of them? ....

    (b)   How many more steps does one of the giants have to take? ....

8 Coming back down the stairs, Patrick shows off and jumps down five at a time. He falls down the last 20 steps. How many jumps did he make before falling? ....

9 Becky and Hayley have British coins of each value and they share them. Becky chooses the coins with odd numbers and Hayley has the coins with even numbers.

    (a)   Which coins do they each have? ....

    (b)   What is the value of Becky's and Hayley's coins? ....

10 Simon eats Smarties ten at a time but Richard eats them in fours. How many mouthfuls will it take each of them to eat 100 Smarties? ....

Unit A3/2 Problems involving rounding and place value

PNS Framework objectives

- Solve one-step and two-step problems involving numbers, money or measures, including time, choosing and carrying out appropriate calculations.
- Multiply one-digit and two-digit numbers by 10 or 100, and describe the effect.
- Round two-digit or three-digit numbers to the nearest 10 or 100 and give estimates for their sums and differences.

Unit learning outcome

- To solve problems involving multiples of 10 and 100.

Prior knowledge

- Understanding of place value (HTUs).
- Understanding of the rules of rounding up or down.

Starter activity

- Children divided up into groups of four to six.

  Each group member takes a handful of cm cubes, counts them, then gives the rest of the group the number rounded to the nearest ten.

  Each group records each member's rounded estimate and totals these to give an estimate of the number of cubes on the table.

  The estimates of each group are collected and totalled on the whiteboard.

  Each group now totals their actual numbers of cubes and these are collected together on the whiteboard alongside their estimates.

  Which groups' estimates were over/under? How close were the estimates?

  Total up the actual numbers for each group and compare it with the estimated total. How close was the class estimate?

  If time allows, repeat using a double handful of cubes.

Answers to A3/2

1   (a) 11   (b) 30   (c) 300
2   (a) 400   (b) 800   (c) 1000
3   (a) Class 1: 467; Class 2: 324; Class 3: 713; Class 4: 692; Class 5: 586; Class 6: 941
     (b) Class 6: 941; Class 3: 713; Class 4: 692; Class 5: 586; Class 1: 467; Class 2: 324
4   (a) Class 1: 500; Class 2: 300; Class 3: 700; Class 4: 700; Class 5: 600; Class 6: 900
     (b) Total: 3700
5   (a) Actual total 3723   (b)   23

Unit A3/2 Problems involving rounding and place value

A crisp company is printing tokens on its packets of crisps. For every 300 collected the school can claim a free book for the library.

Each class staples its tokens together in bundles of ten, and puts ten bundles into every envelope.

1   How many filled envelopes will they need for:

    (a)   1 book? ....   (b)   10 books? ......   (c)   100 books? ....

2   How many tokens would be in:

    (a)   4 envelopes? ......   (b)   8 envelopes? ......   (c)   10 envelopes? ....

3   (a)   After one week this is what each class has collected: how many tokens does each class have?

        Class 1: 4 envelopes, 6 bundles, 7 loose tokens ....
        Class 2: 3 envelopes, 2 bundles, 4 loose tokens ....
        Class 3: 7 envelopes, 1 bundle, 3 loose tokens ....
        Class 4: 6 envelopes, 9 bundles, 2 loose tokens ....
        Class 5: 5 envelopes, 8 bundles, 6 loose tokens ....
        Class 6: 9 envelopes, 4 bundles, 1 loose token ....

    (b)   List the classes and their totals in order, starting with the highest number of tokens.

        ....

4   (a)   What is each class's total rounded to the nearest 100?

        Class 1 ....   Class 2 ....   Class 3 ....
        Class 4 ....   Class 5 ....   Class 6 ....

    (b)   Add up the 'rounded' class totals. ....

5   (a)   Use a calculator to add up the real grand total number of tokens for all the classes.

        ....

    (b)   How close is the estimated (rounded) grand total to the real number? ....

Unit A3/3 Problems involving fractions of a quantity

PNS Framework objectives

- Solve one-step and two-step problems involving numbers, money or measures, including time, choosing and carrying out appropriate calculations.
- Use knowledge of number operations and corresponding inverses, including doubling and halving, to estimate and check calculations.
- Find unit fractions of numbers and quantities (e.g. $\frac{1}{2}$, $\frac{1}{3}$, $\frac{1}{4}$ and $\frac{1}{6}$ of 12 litres).

Unit learning outcome

- To solve problems involving fractions of a quantity.

Prior knowledge

- Know that the result of dividing a number by another is a fraction derived from the divisor, e.g. if you divide 32 by 8 the resulting 4 is one-eighth of 32.
- Able to find non-unit fractions of a number by dividing by the denominator then multiplying by the numerator, e.g. to find $\frac{3}{4}$ of 20, ÷ by 4 then × by 3.

Starter activity

- Divide the class into four groups with equal numbers in each – it may be necessary to either add yourself or class assistant or appoint one of the children as your helper.

  We've divided you all by four so each group is one-fourth, or one-quarter. How many are there of you in one-fourth? How can we find out how many in two- or three-fourths?

  Divide the class by another number, making necessary adjustments to get equal-sized groups and repeat finding non-unit fractions.

  Use the whiteboard to review how you found those non-unit fractions, demonstrating dividing by the denominator to find the unit fraction (e.g. $\frac{1}{4}$ of the number) then multiplying by the numerator to find the non-unit fraction (e.g. $\frac{3}{4}$ of the number).

  Manipulate the total number of children (e.g. by asking someone to hide!) and work through a few more examples on the whiteboard without grouping the children together.

Answers to A3/3

1 (a) 90	(b) 90	(c) 180		**2** (a) 80	(b) 120			
3 (a) 108	(b) 36	(c) 72		**4** (a) 135	(b) 180	(c) 45		
5 (a) 315	(b) 225			**6** (a) 252	(b) 72			
7 (a) 80	(b) 216	(c) 64		**8** (a) 330	(b) 120	(c) 270	(d) 144	
9 (a) 300	(b) 60	(c) 210		**10** 324				

Unit A3/3 Problems involving fractions of a quantity

In a school of 360 children, work out how many children do each of the following:

1. (a) one-quarter go to the library at least once a week ....
   (b) a quarter go sometimes but not as often ....
   (c) the rest do not go to the library at all! ....
2. (a) two-ninths have read at least one Roald Dahl book ....
   (b) one-third have read more than one book by him ....
3. (a) three-tenths like to play football at dinner time ....
   (b) one-tenth think football is a silly game to play ....
   (c) one-fifth prefer to play chasing-around games with their friends ....
4. (a) three-eighths bring packed lunches ....
   (b) one-half stay for school dinners ....
   (c) the rest go home for dinner ....
5. (a) seven-eighths of the children say they would like homework ....
   (b) five-eighths do homework ....
6. (a) seven-tenths think that their teachers are very old ....
   (b) a fifth believe their teachers when they say they're only 21 years old ....
7. (a) two-ninths walk to school on their own ....
   (b) three-fifths walk to school with someone else ....
   (c) the rest are driven to school ....
8. (a) eleven-twelfths would like to be rich and famous ....
   (b) one-third would like to be a footballer ....
   (c) three-quarters would like to be a pop star ....
   (d) two-fifths can sing as badly as their favourite pop star ....
9. (a) five-sixths always put litter in the bin ....
   (b) one-sixth drop litter on the floor ....
   (c) seven-twelfths will tidy up a mess that someone else has made ....
10. Last week one-tenth were off ill, mostly with measles. How many came to school?
    ....

Unit A3/4 One-step and two-step problems

PNS Framework objective

- Solve one-step and two-step problems involving numbers, money or measures, including time, choosing and carrying out appropriate calculations.

Unit learning outcome

- To solve one- and two-step problems involving multiplication.

Prior knowledge

- Able to add, subtract, multiply and divide.

Starter activity

- Play the 'zoo keeper's swapping game'. This is a memory game played around the room in turn. The first player begins with something like 'The zoo keeper had 20 lions so he swapped five of them for ten penguins. Now he has 15 lions and ten penguins.'

  The second player has to pick up from there, e.g. 'The zoo keeper had 15 lions and ten penguins so he swapped two penguins for two ostriches. Now he has 15 lions, eight penguins and two ostriches.'

  Subsequent players continue the swapping. If they wish, they can swap the entire collection of one species of animal; but the resulting trade must be a bigger species.

Answers to A3/4

1	(a) 12	(b) 8	
2	(a) 17	(b) 70	
3	(a) 17	(b) 3	
4	(a) 5 days	(b) 6 days (but then Rover fetches 2 more!)	
5	(a) 60	(b) 8 weeks	(c) 3 bags
6	(a) 3 bags	(b) 8 weeks	(c) 12 bags

Unit A3/4 One-step and two-step problems

1   Jessica buys small dolls with her pocket money. She is hoping to have the complete set of 20. In March she bought the first four, in April another three, and five more in May.

    (a)   How many has she bought so far? ....

    (b)   How many more does she need to complete the set? ....

2   Chris is collecting toy soldiers; he wants to build up an army of 100. He manages to buy 20 in the first week, but can only afford to buy ten a week after that.

    (a)   How many weeks will it take him to complete his 'army'? ....

    (b)   How many had he collected after the fifth week? ....

3   Rover the dog likes to collect sticks from the park. He brought home two on Monday, three on Tuesday, one on Wednesday, two on Thursday, three on Friday and six on Saturday.

    (a)   How many sticks has he got in his collection? ....

    (b)   How many more sticks did he fetch on Sunday to make his collection up to 20? ....

4   Dad decides to throw away five sticks a day while Rover is out.

    (a)   How many days will it take to get rid of them all if Rover doesn't bring any more? ....

    (b)   How many days will it take to get rid of them if Rover brings two more home every day? ....

5   Mum saves her aluminium drinks cans for recycling. She has ten canned drinks a week. She squashes them so that 80 will fit into one bag.

    (a)   How many will she collect in six weeks? ....

    (b)   How long will it take to fill one bag? ....

    (c)   How many bags will she need after 24 weeks? ....

6   The family gets through 30 packets of crisps a week! They buy bags of 20 packets from the supermarket.

    (a)   How many bags do they need every two weeks? ....

    (b)   If they bought ten bags of 24 packets, how long would they last? ....

    (c)   How many bags of 20 packets would last as long as ten bags of 24? ....

Unit A3/5 Addition and subtraction problems

PNS Framework objectives

- Solve one-step and two-step problems involving numbers, money or measures, including time, choosing and carrying out appropriate calculations.
- Mentally add or subtract combinations of one-digit and two-digit numbers.
- Develop and use written methods to record, support or explain addition and subtraction of two-digit and three-digit numbers.

Unit learning outcome

- To solve problems involving addition and subtraction.

Prior knowledge

- Able to carry out 'pencil and paper' addition and subtraction using up to five columns.

Starter activities

- Use newspaper sports pages to examine cricket scores, adding together both innings of each team to decide the winner. Outside the cricket season you can often use the scores of winter-tour test matches.
- Compare the weekly attendance data for the class. *Which was the best week this term so far? Which has been the worst week? What is the difference between the best and worst weeks?*

Answers to A3/5

1 (a) Lancashire by 7 runs   (b) Essex by 1 run   (c) Somerset by 168 runs
2 (a) ordered 1146, bought 1149   (b) 0, 4, 2, 7, 6   (c) 19
3 (a) 1941 miles   (b) 598 miles
4 (a) 30   (b) 38
5 (a) 99   (b) 141

Unit A3/5 Addition and subtraction problems

1   Look at these cricket scores. Total the runs per team and say which team won and by how much.

   (a)   Lancashire: 1st innings 224, 2nd innings 351; Yorkshire: 1st innings 256, 2nd innings 312 ....

   (b)   Surrey: 1st innings 124, 2nd innings 230; Essex: 1st innings 153, 2nd innings 202..........

   (c)   Somerset: 1st innings 325, 2nd innings 234; Kent: 1st innings 199, 2nd innings 192..........

2   A school asks children to order their dinners on a Monday for the rest of the week. Children are sometimes away so the figures usually don't match up.

	Mon.	Tues.	Wed.	Thurs.	Fri.	Total
Ordered	231	231	228	232	224	....
Bought	231	235	226	239	218	....

   (a)   Write in the totals for the week.

   (b)   For each day find out how much the numbers were 'out' – what was the error?
         Mon. ....   Tues. ....   Wed. ....   Thurs. ....   Fri. ....

   (c)   What was the total error for the whole week? ....

3   A family went caravan touring in Europe. When they left home the odometer (milometer) read 33 545, when they returned it read 35 496 miles. They towed the caravan 1353 miles between sites.

   (a)   How far did they drive altogether? ....

   (b)   How far did they drive solo – without the caravan? ....

4   Add up these snooker 'breaks':

   (a)   1 + 7 + 1 + 7 + 1 + 5 + 1 + 6 + 1 ....

   (b)   1 + 7 + 1 + 2 + 2 + 3 + 4 + 5 + 6 + 7 ....

5   Here are the numbers of 'swimmers' in each class:
   Class A 12, Class B 8, Class C 16, Class D 21, Class E 19, Class F 23

   (a)   How many children can swim? ....

   (b)   There are 240 children in the school. How many cannot swim? ....

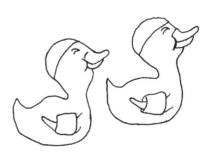

LIVERPOOL JOHN MOORES UNIVERSITY
LEARNING SERVICES

Unit A3/6 Mixed problems

PNS Framework objectives

- Represent the information in a puzzle or problem using numbers, images or diagrams; use these to find a solution and present it in context, where appropriate using £.p notation or units of measure.
- Mentally add or subtract combinations of one-digit and two-digit numbers.

Unit learning outcome

- To solve problems using column addition.

Prior knowledge

- Able to carry out 'pencil and paper' addition, subtraction, multiplication and division in equation format and traditional vertical formats.

Starter activity

- Arrange three two-digit numbers as an equation on one side of the whiteboard and in traditional vertical-addition format on the other side. Ask two volunteers to race against each other to find the answer. Repeat with another set of numbers but with the volunteers switched over. Is one format quicker than the other?

  Try again with four two-digit numbers – discuss if one of the layouts is easier.

  Have similar races to solve subtraction, multiplication and division in equation and vertical formats.

Answers to A3/6

1	(a)	91	(b)	509					
2	(a)	101	(b)	192	(c)	408			
3	(a)	94	(b)	286	(c)	314			
4	(a)	303	(b)	589	(c)	11	(d)	£454.50	
5	(a)	177	(b)	90	(c)	3 days			
6	(a)	£144	(b)	£44					

Unit A3/6 Mixed problems

Phil the dentist counts up how many fillings he does. When he has done 600 he is going to buy a new drill! Work out his weekly totals. It might be easier to add one day at a time.

1   Week 1: Mon. 15, Tues. 24, Wed. 18, Thurs. 22, Fri. 12
    (a)   How many fillings this week? ....
    (b)   How many more does he need before he can buy that new drill? ....

2   Week 2: Mon. 23, Tues. 22, Wed. 20, Thurs. 19, Fri. 17
    (a)   How many fillings this week? ....
    (b)   How many fillings in total so far? ....
    (c)   How many more does he need now to buy that new drill?

3   Week 3: Mon. 21, Tues. 18, Wed. 22, Thurs. 17, Fri. 16
    (a)   How many fillings this week? ....
    (b)   How many fillings in total so far? ....
    (c)   How many more does he need now to buy that new drill? ....

4   Week 4 is 'Children in Need' week. He was sponsored £1.50 for every filling done! Mon. 53, Tues. 62, Wed. 45, Thurs. 56, Fri. 87
    (a)   How many fillings this week? ....
    (b)   How many fillings for the four weeks? ....
    (c)   How many more does he need now to buy that new drill? ....
    (d)   How much did he raise for 'Children in Need'? ....

5   Week 5: 126 of the Week 4 patients complain that their new fillings have fallen out. 36 of them go to a new dentist; the rest agree for him to do the job again, more carefully.
    (a)   How many Week 4 patients did not complain? ....
    (b)   How many fillings does Phil re-fill? ....
    (c)   How long will it take him to do them if he does 30 a day? ....

6   To get new patients he advertises. He could pay £36 a week or £100 for four weeks.
    (a)   What would it cost for four separate weeks? ....
    (b)   How much will he save if he buys the '£100 for four weeks' offer? ....

Unit A3/7 Division problems

PNS Framework objectives

- Solve one-step and two-step problems involving numbers, money or measures, including time, choosing and carrying out appropriate calculations.
- Develop and use written methods to record, support or explain addition and subtraction of two-digit and three-digit numbers.

Unit learning outcome

- To solve problems involving division and remainders.

Prior knowledge

- Able to carry out 'pencil and paper' division involving remainders.

Starter activity

- In groups of four to six, one member collects a double handful of connecting cubes and returns to the group. As soon as you call out a number between three and ten each group races to connect the cubes together in sticks of that number (i.e. in threes, fours, fives, etc.). Any group with no cubes left over has won the round. Record in a table, alongside the number you designated, the number of cubes each group has left over.

  Repeat with a different designated number and the same set of cubes – the previous sticks do not need to be dismantled first. Again a point goes to any group without a remainder.

  Continue until you have tried all the numbers three to ten. Add up the remainders for each group – the group with the lowest remainder is the overall winner.

  Ask each group to count up how many cubes they have been using. Discuss if the number of cubes used has affected the scores.

Answers to A3/7

1	(a) 1	(b) 100	
2	(a) 3	(b) 100	
3	(a) 11	(b) 10	
4	(a) 28	(b) 20	
5	100 boxes of 12 = 1200	(b) none	
6–8	Answers will vary		

Unit A3/7 Division problems

The SafeCo Supermarket is giving away vouchers for schools to collect for 'free' computer equipment. They will give customers one voucher for every whole £30 they spend.

Schools can exchange:

180 vouchers for a printer

900 vouchers for a computer

300 vouchers for a digital camera

35 vouchers for a CD-ROM software disk

90 vouchers for a scanner

10 vouchers for a memory stick

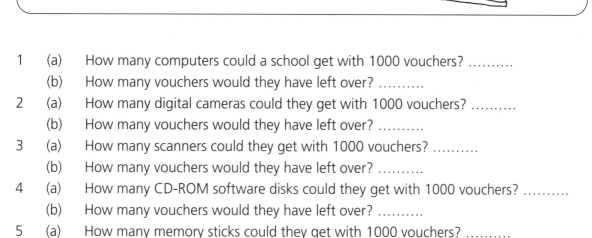

1 (a) How many computers could a school get with 1000 vouchers? ....
   (b) How many vouchers would they have left over? ....
2 (a) How many digital cameras could they get with 1000 vouchers? ....
   (b) How many vouchers would they have left over? ....
3 (a) How many scanners could they get with 1000 vouchers? ....
   (b) How many vouchers would they have left over? ....
4 (a) How many CD-ROM software disks could they get with 1000 vouchers? ....
   (b) How many vouchers would they have left over? ....
5 (a) How many memory sticks could they get with 1000 vouchers? ....
   (b) How many vouchers would they have left over? ....

How can these schools use their vouchers? 'Spend' as many of their vouchers as you can.

6 Billinge School has collected 530 vouchers.
   (a) What could they buy? ....
   (b) How many vouchers will they have left over? ....
7 Priory School has collected 949 vouchers.
   (a) What could they buy? ....
   (b) How many vouchers will they have left over? ....
8 The Rowland School has collected 1489 vouchers.
   (a) What could they buy? ....
   (b) How many vouchers will they have left over? ....

Unit A3/8 Problems involving doubling

PNS Framework objectives

- Identify patterns and relationships involving numbers or shapes, and use these to solve problems.
- Mentally add or subtract combinations of one-digit and two-digit numbers.

Unit learning outcome

- To solve problems involving doubling.

Prior knowledge

- Able to carry out 'pencil and paper' division involving remainders.

Starter activities

- Arrange the children in groups or pairs, each with a calculator and a piece of paper for recording results. The objective is to see how many times they can multiply by the same factor before the calculator display runs out of room. Each pair begins with 2, key in to the calculator 2 × = then continue to press =, counting each press, until the display runs out of space. Record the number of presses for 2. Repeat for 3, 4, 5, 6, 7, 8, 9 and 10. When complete, check to see if everyone had the same answers – did everyone have a calculator with the same number of character spaces on the screen?

- Arrange as per activity 1 with squared paper for recording. Each pair begins with 2, key in to the calculator 2 × = and continue to press =, writing down the number displayed on the screen each time in a column, then continue. When they have a column of × 2, clear the calculator and do the same using 4 × =, stopping when they reach the same number as the last one in the 2s column. Look at the two columns of numbers and match up where the same numbers appear in both columns.

Answers to A3/8

1	(a)	80 cm	(b)	160 cm	(c)	320 cm		
2	(a)	4 cm	(b)	16 cm	(c)	64 cm	(d)	Tuesday
3	(a)	14 cm	(b)	28 cm	(c)	55 cm	(d)	112 cm
4	(a)	380 cm	(b)	240 cm	(c)	120 cm	(d)	60 cm
	(e)	30 cm	(f)	15 cm	(g)	$7\frac{1}{2}$ cm		

Unit A3/8 Problems involving doubling

Last week Chris was kidnapped by aliens. When they grew tired of his singing (after ten minutes) they brought him back to Earth and gave him a present called 'Special Growth Tonic'.

On Monday night he gave some to his hamster. Harry the hamster was his usual 10 cm long on Monday morning.

By Tuesday night he had doubled in length to 20 cm. Chris had to let him out of the cage and put him in the shed.

By Wednesday night Harry had doubled again to 40 cm long, and the dog was looking worried!

1 (a) How long was Harry the hamster on Thursday? ....
  (b) How long was he on Friday, the same day the dog left home? ....
  (c) How long was he on Saturday, when he moved into the garage? ....

Chris mixed some tonic in his dad's hair shampoo bottle.

Dad's hair had just been cut and was just 1 cm long! He washed his hair on Monday night which made his hair double in length every day.

2 (a) How long was it by Wednesday night? ....
  (b) How long was it by Friday night? ....
  (c) How long was it on Sunday night? ....
  (d) Dad is two metres tall. What day will his hair reach the floor? ....

Chris is worried. He pours the rest of the tonic away, over the front lawn!

The day before, the grass had been 7 cm long.

3 How long was the grass after:
  (a) one day? ....
  (b) two days? ....
  (c) three days? ....
  (d) four days? ....

Chris woke up to the sound of a five-metre-long hamster eating the grass. By 1 o'clock it was just 960 cm long. Harry ate half the length of the grass each hour.

4 How long was the grass at:
  (a) 2 o'clock? ....
  (b) 4 o'clock? ....
  (c) 6 o'clock? ....
  (d) 8 o'clock? ....

Unit A3/9 Problems involving multiplication of money

PNS Framework objectives

- Solve one-step and two-step problems involving numbers, money or measures, including time, choosing and carrying out appropriate calculations.
- Represent the information in a puzzle or problem using numbers, images or diagrams; use these to find a solution and present it in context, where appropriate using £.p notation or units of measure.

Unit learning outcome

- To solve problems involving multiplication short cuts.

Prior knowledge

- Able to make approximations by rounding figures.
- Able to use mental shortcuts (e.g. rounding then adjusting).
- Able to carry out 'pencil and paper' multiplication.

Starter activity

- As a class, measure the height and width of the classroom walls and work out the area of each, remembering to subtract the area of any doors and windows within them.

    Work out the amount of paint required to cover the walls – a typical figure would be 1 litre per 4 m². Use mental shortcuts where applicable.

    Work out the cost of the required paint at £21 per 5 litre can, taking into account that the paint has to be bought in units of 5 litres so some will be left over.

Answers to A3/9

1	(a)	£6	(b)	£14	(c)	£34	(d)	£119.80	
	(e)	£27.50	(f)	£18.45	(g)	£17.55	(h)	£1.50	
2	(a)	£10.80	(b)	£3.98	(c)	£15.75	(d)	£175	
3	$47\frac{1}{2}$ hours								
4	£980								
5	(a)	£119.50	(b)	£66	(c)	£50.50	(d)	£330	
6	(a)	£136.50	(b)	£134.40	(c)	£99.50	(d)	£76.65	
	(e)	£540	(f)	51.80					

Unit A3/9 Problems involving multiplication of money

Use multiplication short-cuts to solve these problems. Try to do them in your head.

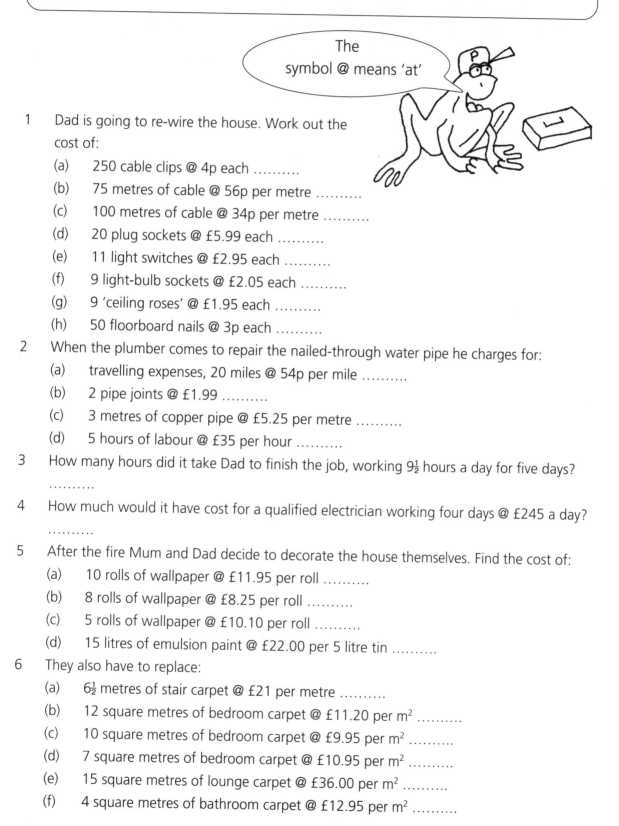

The symbol @ means 'at'

1   Dad is going to re-wire the house. Work out the cost of:
    (a)   250 cable clips @ 4p each ....
    (b)   75 metres of cable @ 56p per metre ....
    (c)   100 metres of cable @ 34p per metre ....
    (d)   20 plug sockets @ £5.99 each ....
    (e)   11 light switches @ £2.95 each ....
    (f)   9 light-bulb sockets @ £2.05 each ....
    (g)   9 'ceiling roses' @ £1.95 each ....
    (h)   50 floorboard nails @ 3p each ....

2   When the plumber comes to repair the nailed-through water pipe he charges for:
    (a)   travelling expenses, 20 miles @ 54p per mile ....
    (b)   2 pipe joints @ £1.99 ....
    (c)   3 metres of copper pipe @ £5.25 per metre ....
    (d)   5 hours of labour @ £35 per hour ....

3   How many hours did it take Dad to finish the job, working $9\frac{1}{2}$ hours a day for five days?
    ....

4   How much would it have cost for a qualified electrician working four days @ £245 a day?
    ....

5   After the fire Mum and Dad decide to decorate the house themselves. Find the cost of:
    (a)   10 rolls of wallpaper @ £11.95 per roll ....
    (b)   8 rolls of wallpaper @ £8.25 per roll ....
    (c)   5 rolls of wallpaper @ £10.10 per roll ....
    (d)   15 litres of emulsion paint @ £22.00 per 5 litre tin ....

6   They also have to replace:
    (a) $6\frac{1}{2}$ metres of stair carpet @ £21 per metre ....
    (b)   12 square metres of bedroom carpet @ £11.20 per m² ....
    (c)   10 square metres of bedroom carpet @ £9.95 per m² ....
    (d)   7 square metres of bedroom carpet @ £10.95 per m² ....
    (e)   15 square metres of lounge carpet @ £36.00 per m² ....
    (f)   4 square metres of bathroom carpet @ £12.95 per m² ....

Unit A3/10 Bar graphs, Venn and Carroll diagrams

PNS Framework objectives

- Follow a line of enquiry by deciding what information is important; make and use lists, tables and graphs to organise and interpret the information.
- Use Venn diagrams or Carroll diagrams to sort data and objects using more than one criterion.

Unit learning outcome

- To interpret bar graphs and Venn and Carroll diagrams.

Prior knowledge

- This unit reinforces work from Units D3/2–4.
- Familiar with the principles of Venn and Carroll diagrams.
- Able to read information from a bar chart.

Starter activity

- Each pupil makes a small name label for themselves.

  Lay two large, overlapping Venn rings on a table (or draw on the whiteboard) and label them 'likes tea' and 'likes coffee'.

  Invite pupils to place their name label in the sector that corresponds to their preference(s). Some may need to put their label outside the rings. How many like tea and coffee, how many like only tea/coffee?

  Repeat a couple more times using 'likes' labels for in vogue pop singers, sports, TV programmes, etc.

Answers to A3/10

1. (a) 9　(b) 8　(c) 7　(d) 3　(e) 5　(f) 4
2. (a) Children's　(b) News
3. 36
4. (a) 8　(b) 8　(c) 3　(d) Cat, dog　(e) Caterpillar
5. Various answers possible
6. (a) Two of: Oslo, Walsall, Lyon, Rome, Berne, Bruges
   (b) Two of: Cairo, Tokyo, New York, Lima, Tripoli, Karachi
   (c) Three of: Canada, Brazil, Thailand, India, Korea, China
   (d) Three of: France, Italy, Belgium, Spain, Britain, Germany
   (e) Belgium, Britain, Brazil
7. Various answers possible

Unit A3/10 Bar graphs, Venn and Carroll diagrams

On this page there is a bar chart, a Venn diagram and a Carroll diagram. You will need to study them carefully to answer the questions on this page.

1   How many children like to watch:
    (a)   children's programmes? ....
    (b)   comedy? ....
    (c)   films? ....   (e)   soaps? ....
    (d)   news? ....   (f)   sport? ......

2   Which type of programme is:
    (a)   most popular? ....
    (b)   least popular? ....

3   How many children took part in the survey?
    ....

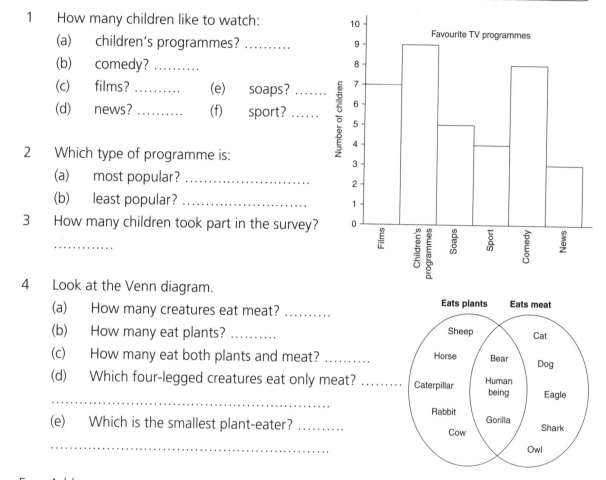

4   Look at the Venn diagram.
    (a)   How many creatures eat meat? ....
    (b)   How many eat plants? ....
    (c)   How many eat both plants and meat? ....
    (d)   Which four-legged creatures eat only meat? ....
    ....
    (e)   Which is the smallest plant-eater? ....
    ....

5   Add some more creatures to the diagram. You may need to check what they eat.

6   Name:
    (a)   two towns in Europe ....
    ....
    (b)   two towns not in Europe ....
    ....
    (c)   three non-European countries ....
    ....
    (d)   three European countries ....
    (e)   three countries that begin with B ....

	In Europe		Not in Europe	
Country	France Italy		Canada Brazil	
	Belgium Spain		Thailand India	
	Britain Germany		Korea China	
Towns (and cities)	Oslo Walsall		Cairo Tokyo	
	Lyon Rome		New York Lima	
	Berne Bruges		Tripoli Karachi	

7   Use an atlas and add more countries and towns to your own version of the Carroll diagram.

Unit A3/11 Problems involving capacity, volume and mass

PNS Framework objectives

- Solve one-step and two-step problems involving numbers, money or measures, including time, choosing and carrying out appropriate calculations.
- Know the relationships between kilometres and metres, metres and centimetres, kilograms and grams, litres and millilitres; choose and use appropriate units to estimate, measure and record measurements.

Unit learning outcome

- To solve problems involving capacity, volume and mass.

Prior knowledge

- This unit reinforces work from Units M3/1–3.
- Familiar with units for capacity, length and mass.
- Competent with basic computation with all four functions.

Starter activity

- Play 'Unit Snap'. For this you need to make two separate sets of cards, one set marked with units of measurement (m, cm, mm, l, ml, g, kg) and another marked with products that might be sold by a measured amount: e.g. sweets, pop, fabric, potatoes, squash, wrapping paper, etc. The more cards in each set the better.

  Both sets of cards are shuffled and placed face down. Divide the class/group into two teams, each responsible for one of the sets of cards. On a count of one, two, three a member of each team simultaneously turns over the top card. (Team members take turns at doing this.) If the unit is appropriate for measuring the product, e.g. ml or l matched with pop, then it is a 'snap!' and whichever team calls out first wins a point. False 'snaps!' lose a point. When both sets of cards have been turned over they are each shuffled and the teams swap sets and play continues.

  Continue to play either up to a specified number of points, or for a predetermined time.

Answers to A3/11

1	(a)	22 l	(b)	9.5 l	(c)	12.56 l	(d)	17.75 l	
2	(a)	2200 ml	(b)	9500 ml	(c)	12560 ml	(d)	17750 ml	
3	(a)	3300 ml	(b)	45500 ml	(c)	42440 ml	(d)	37250 ml	
4	(a)	1000 cm	(b)	62	(c)	50	(d)	125	
5	(a)	2 litre bottles (costs 47.5p per litre)	(b)	5.33	(c)	5.5 l	(d)	8 litres
6	(a)	£10.20	(b)	£9.90	(c)	500 g	(d)	1250 g	
	(e)	1000 g	(f)	1000 g					

Unit A3/11 Problems involving capacity, volume and mass

1   Phil Ittup's car has a fuel tank with a capacity of 55
     litres. He always fills the tank up when he buys fuel.
     How much was left in the tank if he has to put in:
     (a)   33 litres? ....
     (b)   45.5 litres? ....
     (c)   42.44 litres? ....
     (d)   37.25 litres? ....

2   Change the litres left in the tank in question 1 into millilitres.
     (a)   ....   (b)   ....   (c)   ....   (d)   ....

3   Change the litres put in the tank in question 1 into millilitres.
     (a)   ....   (b)   ....   (c)   ....   (d)   ....

4   Sweeny's sausage machine makes one giant ten-metre-long sausage which has to be
     split up into normal-sized sausages.
     (a)   How many centimetres long is the giant sausage? ....
     (b)   How many 16 cm sausages could he get from it? ....
     (c)   How many 20 cm sausages could he get from it? ....
     (d)   How many 8 cm sausages could he get from it? ....

5   SafeCo supermarket sells pop in these sizes:

     SafeCo supermarket
     special offers on drinks
     330 ml cans 25p
     half-litre bottles 35p
     2 litre bottles 95p

     (a)   Which is the cheapest price per litre? ....
     (b)   How many litres of pop could you buy for £4.00 in cans? ....
     (c)   How many litres of pop could you buy for £4.00 in half-litre bottles? ....
     (d)   How many litres of pop could you buy for £4.00 in 2 litre bottles? ....

6   SafeCo supermarket sells bags of sweets in these sizes:

     SafeCo supermarket
     supa sweets!
     250 g for 85p
     500 g for £1.65
     1 kg for £3.40

     (a)   How much would it cost to buy 3 kg of sweets in
            250 g bags? ....
     (b)   How much would it cost to buy 3 kg of sweets in
            500 g bags? ....
     (c)   Which size of bag gives the best value? ....
     (d)   How many grams of sweets could you buy with £4.50, buying in 250 g bags?
            ....
     (e)   How many grams of sweets could you buy with £4.50, buying in 500 g bags?
            ....
     (f)   How many grams of sweets could you buy with £4.50, buying in 1 kg bags?
            ....

Unit A3/12 Problems involving time

PNS Framework objectives

- Describe and explain methods, choices and solutions to puzzles and problems, orally and in writing, using pictures and diagrams.
- Read the time on a 12-hour digital clock and to the nearest five minutes on an analogue clock; calculate time intervals and find start or end times for a given time interval.

Unit learning outcome

- To solve problems involving time.

Prior knowledge

- This unit follows/reinforces work from Units M3/4 to 6.
- Able to work out time intervals on paper.
- Able to add up periods of time on paper.

Starter activity

- Demonstrate then practise the counting-on method of working out time intervals as per this example:

     09:40 to 11:15

    09:40 to 10:00 = 20 minutes
    10:00 to 11:00 = 1 hour
    11:00 to 11:15 = 15 minutes
    Total time = 1 hour and 35 minutes

- Demonstrate then practise the counting-on method of working out time intervals as per this example:

	Hours	Mins
	0	60
Exchange 1 hour for 60 minutes	1̸0̸	15
Subtract 40 mins from the 60 mins	9	40
then add on the 15 mins		
Subtract 9 hours from 10 hours	1	35

- Demonstrate adding up time intervals similarly, dividing minutes by 60 to find hours to exchange and leaving the remainder in the minutes column.

Answers to A3/12

1 and **2** Various answers depending upon the day

3 (a) 15 days   (b) 08:05 (out) and 05:30 (return)   (c) 1 hour 45 minutes   (d) 09:05

4 (a) 7:25–8:05   (b) 6:20–7:15   (c) 8:10–9:35

5 (a) 15 minutes   (b) 500 seconds = 8 minutes 20 seconds

6 (a) 1 hour 45 minutes   (b) 9:15

7 33 minutes eating, 187 minutes (3 hours 7 minutes) 'hunting', 20 hours 20 minutes sleeping

Unit A3/12 Problems involving time

1 (a) What was the date ten days ago? ....
   (b) What day did it fall on? ....
2 (a) What day will it be in ten days time? ....
   (b) What day will it fall on? ....
3 Rachel is going on holiday. She is leaving on 26th July and returning on 10th August. The flight out takes off at 9:55 and lands at 11:40. The return flight takes off at 7:20.
   (a) How long is she going to be away for? ....
   (b) She has to check in at the airport 1 hour and 50 minutes before each flight. What times will these be?
        Outward flight ....
        Return flight ....
   (c) How long does the flight out last? ....
   (d) The return flight will take the same length of time. When will it land? ....
4 Before going away she set the video to record her favourite programmes. She added on 5 minutes to the start and end of the recording time. What start and stop times did she use for:
   (a) a 30 minute programme due to start at 7:30? ....
   (b) a 45 minute programme due to start at 6:25? ....
   (c) a 75 minute programme due to start at 8:15? ....
5 Chris enters a pie-eating contest. It takes him $1\frac{1}{2}$ minutes to eat his first pie.
   (a) How long might it take him to eat ten? ....
   (b) He finds each pie takes five seconds longer than the one before it. How long does it take to eat five pies? ....
6 After recovering Chris goes to the gym. He spends ten minutes warming up, 70 minutes exercising, five minutes cooling down and 20 minutes showering and getting changed.
   (a) How long did he spend at the gym? ....
   (b) If he arrived at 7:30, what time did he leave?
        ....

7 Ratbag the cat only seems to do three things all day. How long does he spend altogether doing each activity?
   (a) Eating: 7:30 till 7:40, 12:00 till 12:07, 5:45 till 5:55 and 10:05 till 10:11 ....
   (b) 'Hunting': 7:40 till 8:30, 12:10 till 12:50, 5:05 till 5:54 and 10:12 till 11:00 ....
   (c) Sleeping for the rest of the day (remember there are 24 hours in a day) ....

Unit A3/13 Problems involving direction and turn

PNS Framework objectives

- Describe and explain methods, choices and solutions to puzzles and problems, orally and in writing, using pictures and diagrams.
- Read and record the vocabulary of position, direction and movement, using the four compass directions to describe movement about a grid.

Unit learning outcome

- To solve problems involving direction and turn.

Prior knowledge

- This unit reinforces work from Units M3/4 and 6.
- Know that a quarter turn is a right angle and that four right angles make one complete turn.
- Familiar with the four-point compass.

Starter activity

- Play 'Blindfold Remote Control' – the object is to guide a pupil who has their eyes shut around the room using verbal instructions.

  The volunteer is put in a starting position, and without them seeing, the intended stopping position is identified. Pupils take it in turns to give an instruction choosing from 'forwards one step', 'backwards one step', 'turn one right angle to the right' and 'turn one right angle to the left'.

  The pupil who gives the final, successful instruction swaps places with the volunteer and is then guided to a new position in the classroom.

Answers to A3/13

1   (a) west   (b) 3

2   (a) right, right, left   (b) left, left, right

3   (a) 4   (b) 3 hours   (c) 15 minutes   (d) 9 hours

      (e) 45 minutes

4   (a) 8   (b) 96

5   (a) 20   (b) 24

6   (a) move/dive/turn the opposite direction

      (b) the torpedo will come around in a circle and hit the submarine (yes, this was an acknowledged risk!)

Unit A3/13 Problems involving direction and turn

1   A car is travelling north when it turns off left.

    (a)   What direction is it now travelling in? ....

    (b)   How many more left turns does it need to make before it is travelling north again?

           ....

2   The driver is going the wrong way; he wants to go south instead of north.

    (a)   If he takes the next turning on the right, which way does he turn at the next three junctions to get back on the right road? ....

    (b)   If he takes the next turning on the left, which way does he turn at the next three junctions to get back on the right road? ....

3   (a)   How many right angles are there on a clock face? ....

    (b)   How long does it take the hour hand to turn through one right angle? ....

    (c)   How long does it take the minute hand to turn through one right angle? ....

    (d)   How long does it take the hour hand to turn through three right angles? ....

    (e)   How long does it take the minute hand to turn through three right angles? ....

4   During a whole day (24 hours):

    (a)   how many right angles does the hour hand turn through? ....

    (b)   how many right angles does the minute hand turn through? ....

5   Darren is making a lidless box out of wooden panels. Each square needs metal corner pieces to make it stronger.

    (a)   How many metal corner pieces does he need? ....

    (b)   If he makes a lid as well, how many corner pieces will he need? ....

6   A submarine fires a torpedo. The captain sees that the torpedo isn't going straight; it's turning left in a large circle.

    (a)   What should the submarine captain do? ....

    (b)   What will happen if he doesn't do anything? ....

    (c)   Use a book or pencil case on your desk to represent the submarine. Pretend your pencil is the torpedo being fired and turning around to the left all the time. Were you right with your answer to 6(b)? ....

Unit A4/1 Problems involving place value and rounding

PNS Framework objectives

- Solve one-step and two-step problems involving numbers, money or measures, including time; choose and carry out appropriate calculations, using calculator methods where appropriate.
- Use knowledge of rounding, number operations and inverses to estimate and check calculations.

Unit learning outcome

- Problems involving place value and rounding.

Prior knowledge

- Knows that zero has no value of its own but affects the value of other numerals.
- Understands the basic principle of rounding, up if the figure to the right is =5, down if the figure to the right is ≤4.

Starter activities

- Make a three-digit number out of numeral cards on the whiteboard – What number is it? Slide two digits over to the left and insert a zero to the right – What number do we have now? Try the zero in different positions in relation to the other three digits. Discuss the effect of the zero. Try with other digits and adding a pair of zeros.
- Measure a few people's pencils in cm to the nearest mm and write the measurements down with a decimal point. Ask if it's important to have such an accurate measure. *Let's put the lengths down to the nearest whole centimetre.* Draw a section of number line showing 1 mm divisions – *Which whole number is it closest to?* Introduce the rounding rule, five or more round up, otherwise ignore.

Answers to A4/1

1	(a)	£53.35, £4950	(b)	£87.26, £783	(c)	£65.25, £5985
	(d)	£103.87, £927	(e)	£85.65, £84 915		
2	(a)	85 368, 85 371, 3 miles	(b)	85 371, 85 375, 4 miles	(c)	85 375, 85 380, 5 miles
	(d)	85 380, 85 384, 4 miles	(e)	85 384, 85 388, 4 miles	(f)	85 388, 85 393, 5 miles
	(g)	25 miles	(h)	85 392.6 – 85 367.6 = 25 miles		
	(i)	yes				
3	(a)	1.5	(b)	4	(c)	2.5
	(d)	2	(e)	1.5	(f)	3

Unit A4/1 Problems involving place value and rounding

1   A fuel company's computer keeps adding in extra 0s to the bills it sends to customers. Luckily the extra 0s are in bold print. Remove them and complete the following:

(a)   The bill asks for £5**00**3.35. It should say ………. It is asking for ………. too much.

(b)   The bill asks for £870.26**00**. It should say ………. It is asking for ………. too much.

(c)   The bill asks for £**0**6050.25. It should say ………. It is asking for ………. too much.

(d)   The bill asks for £103**0**.87. It should say ………. It is asking for ………. too much.

(e)   The bill asks for £85**000**.65. It should say ………. It is asking for ………. too much.

2   A school is planning a sponsored bicycle ride and needs to know how far each stage is. The head teacher measures it in his car but the milometer includes tenths of a mile. Round his milometer readings to the nearest whole mile and work out how far each stage is.

(a)   Stage 1 starts at 85 367.6 finishes at 85 371.3 distance = ………. miles

(b)   Stage 2 starts at 85 371.3 finishes at 85 375.1 distance = ………. miles

(c)   Stage 3 starts at 85 375.1 finishes at 85 379.9 distance = ………. miles

(d)   Stage 4 starts at 85 379.9 finishes at 85 384.4 distance = ………. miles

(e)   Stage 5 starts at 85 384.4 finishes at 85 387.8 distance = ………. miles

(f)   Stage 6 starts at 85 387.8 finishes at 85 392.6 distance = ………. miles

(g)   The total distance of all six stages is ………. miles

(h)   Use a calculator to find the actual distance covered by the head's car by subtracting 85 367.6 from 85 392.6 ……….

(i)   Are the distances for (g) and (h) the same? ……….

3   Dad is going to put up some new curtain tracks, but Mum hasn't told him yet. The shop sells tracks in these lengths: 1 m, 1.5 m, 2 m, 2.5 m, 3 m and 4 m. Decide which length of track Mum will need to buy for each window.

(a)   The bathroom window is 1.3 m wide. Mum needs to buy a ……….m length of track.

(b)   The lounge window is 3.1 m wide. Mum needs to buy a ……….m length of track.

(c)   The kitchen window is 2.3 m wide. Mum needs to buy a ……….m length of track.

(d)   The bedroom window is 1.9 m wide. Mum needs to buy a ……….m length of track.

(e)   The landing window is 1.3 m wide. Mum needs to buy a ……….m length of track.

(f)   The spare room window is 2.6 m wide. Mum needs to buy a ……….m length of track.

Unit A4/2 Problems with number sequences, multiplication, squaring and square roots

PNS Framework objectives

- Identify and use patterns, relationships and properties of numbers or shapes; investigate a statement involving numbers and test it with examples.
- Recognise and continue number sequences formed by counting on or back in steps of constant size.

Unit learning outcome

- Problems involving number sequences, multiplication, squaring and square roots.

Prior knowledge

- Able to count in twos.
- Knows common times tables including square numbers.

Starter activities

- (Before starting Q1) Jumping frogs – you need a sequence of numbered lily pads drawn on the whiteboard or large sheet of paper on a table. Place your 'frog' on a lily pad – How many jumps will it take to get from here to here? Try again from different starting points before introducing superfrog – he jumps over every other lily pad! If he starts here, which lily pads will he land on to get over here?
- (Before starting Q3) On squared paper draw and colour squares made of 2 × 2, 3 × 3, 4 × 4 squares, etc. Point out that the first has two rows of two, the second has three rows of three, etc. *How many little squares are there in each?* Introduce and explain the terms 'square number' and squared.

    Explain that when we reverse the squaring process we are finding the 'square root'. Demonstrate by reversing the squaring – 9 divided by 3 = 3 so the square root of 9 is 3, etc.

Answers to A4/2

1	(a) 1, 3, 5, 7, 9, 11	(b) 11, 9, 7, 5, 3, 1	(c) 2, 4, 6, 8, 10
	(d) 10, 8, 6, 4, 2	(e) 2, 5, 8, 11	(f) 10, 7, 4, 1
2	(a) 25 pairs	(b) 2500 pairs	(c) 200 baseball caps
	(d) 500 pairs of gloves		
3	(a) 36 cheese rolls	(b) 9 pies	(c) 100 peanuts
	(d) 49 bananas		
4	(a) 5 sticks of rock	(b) 10 Manchester United shirts	(c) 8 money boxes
	(d) 4 T-shirts		

Unit A4/2 Problems with number sequences, multiplication, squaring and square roots

1   The paving slabs of the path from school to the playground have been numbered by a
     mad maths teacher. Number 1 is by the door and number 11 is by the playground. Some
     of the children prefer to leap instead of walk.
     Danielle uses the first slab then jumps over every other slab.
     (a)   Which slabs does she use when she goes out for playtime? ....
     (b)   Which slabs does she use when she comes back in? ....
     Liam jumps over the first slab and lands on every other one.
     (c)   Which slabs does he jump on when he goes out for playtime? ....
     (d)   Which slabs does he jump on when he comes back in? ....
     Jak jumps onto the second slab then jumps over two at a time.
     (e)   Which slabs does he use when he goes out for playtime? ....
     (f)   Which slabs does he use when he comes back in? ....

2   A party of 100 aliens are planning to visit Earth. They
     need to disguise themselves. They each have two
     heads, each with 50 eyes, five legs and feet, and ten
     arms and hands.

   (a)   How many pairs of sunglasses will each alien
          need? ....
   (b)   How many pairs of sunglasses will be needed
          for the whole group? ....
   (c)   How many baseball caps will they need altogether? ....
   (d)   How many pairs of gloves will they need to buy to fit all of them? ....

3   They have brought a machine with them. Whatever is put inside is multiplied by itself.
     What will come out of the machine if they put in:
     (a)   six cheese rolls? ....
     (b)   three pies? ....
     (c)   ten peanuts? ....
     (d)   seven bananas? ....

4   They buy too many souvenirs for the flying saucer to take off. They set the machine on
     reverse so that it reduces things to their square root. What will they get out when they
     put in:
     (a)   25 sticks of rock? ....
     (b)   100 Manchester United shirts? ....
     (c)   64 money boxes shaped like a London bus? ....
     (d)   16 cheap-looking T-shirts? ....

Unit A4/3 Problems involving place value and decimal points

PNS Framework objective

- Solve one-step and two-step problems involving numbers, money or measures, including time; choose and carry out appropriate calculations, using calculator methods where appropriate.

Unit learning outcome

- Problems involving place value and decimal points.

Prior knowledge

- Understanding of place value.
- Understanding that the decimal point marks the boundary between whole numbers and fractions.

Starter activities

- Use the place-value multiplier (as illustrated in M3/2) in conjunction with numerals written up on the whiteboard to multiply and divide them by 10 and 100. Point out that the decimal point is usually used only if there are numerals worth less than 1.
- Write down sums of money as both £ and as p, stressing that only one symbol is used. Use the place-value multiplier to convert £ to p and vice versa, noting the position of the decimal point.

Answers to A4/3

1	(a) £1.10	(b) £1.35	(c) £1.80	(d) £0.75	(e) £4.20
2	(a) £108.90	(b) £133.65	(c) £178.20	(d) £74.25	(e) £415.80
3	(a) £18.95	(b) £39.85	(c) £35.50	(d) £29.45	
4	(a) £550.49	(b) £678.50	(c) £220.67	(d) £239.99	
5	100 times larger				
6	(a) 1.95 m	(b) 3.50 m	(c) 2 m long, 1.50 m wide, 1.85 m tall		
	(d) 8 m long, 2.25 m wide, 2.85 m tall				
7	(a) 193.05 m	(b) 346.5 m			
	(c) 198 m too long, 148.5 m too wide, 183.15 m too tall				
	(d) 792 m too long, 222.75 m too wide, 282.15 m too tall				
8	100 times larger				

Unit A4/3 Problems involving place value and decimal points

When this page was printed all the decimal points were missed off.

1   These prices are all wrong because the decimal points are missing. Write down the correct prices, they all cost less than £10.
   (a)   A bag of chips £110 ....
   (b)   A cheese and onion pasty £135 ....
   (c)   A chicken portion £180 ....
   (d)   A can of pop £75 ....
   (e)   Fish and chips £420 ....

2   Find the difference between the printed prices in question 1 and the real prices.
   (a)   £110 – .... = ...
   (b)   £135 – .... = ...
   (c)   £180 – .... = ...
   (d)   £75 – .... = ...
   (e)   £420 – .... = ...

3   Use a decimal point to find the correct prices of these things. They all cost more than £10 but less than £100.
   (a)   Hair drier £1895 ....
   (b)   MP3 player £3985 ....
   (c)   Electric kettle £3550 ....
   (d)   Electric toaster £2945 ....

4   Try the same with these, they all cost more than £100 but less than £1000.
   (a)   Laptop computer £55049 ....
   (b)   Wide-screen television £67850 ....
   (c)   Vacuum cleaner £22067 ....
   (d)   Washing machine £23999 ....

5   How many times bigger are the printed prices than the correct ones? ....

6   The decimal points have been missed off these measurements. Give the correct sizes.
   (a)   Classroom door 195 m tall ....
   (b)   Patio window 350 m wide ....
   (c)   Tool shed 200 m long, 150 m wide and 185 m tall .... long, ... wide, ...tall
   (d)   Garage 800 m long, 225 m wide and 285 m tall .... long, ... wide, ... tall

7   Find the difference between the printed sizes and the real ones.
   (a)   195 m – .... = ...
   (b)   350 m – .... = ...
   (c)   200 m – .... = ...
         150 m – .... = ...
         185 m – .... = ...
   (d)   800 m – .... = ...
         225 m – .... = ...
         285 m – .... = ...

8   How many times bigger are the printed sizes than the correct ones?

Unit A4/4 Problems involving two steps

PNS Framework objective

- Solve one-step and two-step problems involving numbers, money or measures, including time; choose and carry out appropriate calculations, using calculator methods where appropriate.

Unit learning outcome

- Problems involving two steps.

Prior knowledge

- Able to use pencil and paper computation.
- Able to interpret how to find the answers.

Starter activities

- Brainstorm things that are often bought in multiple packs: e.g. yoghurts, fish fingers, eggs, crayons, matches, drawing pins, etc., and stipulate how many you might have in the pack. *How many would you have of each if you bought 2/3/4/5 packs?*
- Discuss and estimate how many packs of pencils your class will use in a year. Use this to estimate how many packs the whole school might get through. Do the same for other items such as handwriting pens, crayons, whiteboard pens, etc.

Answers to A4/4

1	(a) 240	(b) 250	(c) 310	(d) 130
	(e) 120	(f) 250	(g) 110	(h) 210
2	(a) 50 red	(b) 110 blue	(c) 390 brown	(d) 120 green
	(e) 310 orange	(f) 640 black	(g) 1620 altogether	
3	900 paper clips			
4	144 pens			

Unit A4/4 Problems involving two steps

The deputy headteacher is doing a stock take. He is finding out who has got what. He asks for details of full boxes only.

1   Pencil crayons are in boxes of 10, how many are there in each class?
    (a)   Nursery has 4 boxes of red, 1 of blue, 6 each of brown and orange, 2 of green, 5 of black ....
    (b)   Reception has 1 box of red, 3 of blue, 6 each of brown, orange and black, 3 of green ....
    (c)   Class 1 has 5 boxes of blue, 8 of brown, 4 of green, 5 of orange and 9 of black ....
    (d)   Class 2 has 2 boxes of blue, 4 of brown, 1 of green, 2 of orange and 4 of black ....
    (e)   Class 3 has 1 box of brown, 2 of green, 3 of orange and 6 of black ....
    (f)   Class 4 has 8 boxes of brown, 7 of orange and 10 of black ....
    (g)   Class 5 has 2 boxes of orange and 9 of black ....
    (h)   Class 6 has 6 boxes of brown and 15 of black ....

2   How many boxed crayons has he found of each colour?
    (a)   Red ....   (b)   Blue ....   (c)   Brown ....
    (d)   Green ....   (e)   Orange ....   (f)   Black ....
    (g)   How many boxed crayons has he found altogether? ....

3   He decided to find out how many paper clips there are in school. There are 100 in a box. He found 2 boxes in the secretary's office, 6 boxes in the head teacher's cupboard, 1 box in Key Stage 1 and none at all in key Stage 2.

    How many boxed paper clips are there altogether? ....

4   He checked how many handwriting pens Key Stage 2 have to the nearest half box. A full box holds 12 pens.

    He found 2 boxes in Year 3, $3\frac{1}{2}$ boxes in Year 4, 4 boxes in Year 5 and $2\frac{1}{2}$ boxes in Year 6.

    How many handwriting pens did he find? ....

Unit A4/5 Problems involving interpreting frequency tables

PNS Framework objective

- Suggest a line of enquiry and the strategy needed to follow it; collect, organise and interpret selected information to find answers.

Unit learning outcome

- Problems involving interpreting frequency tables.

Prior knowledge

- Able to add and subtract HTUs in columns.
- Able to read data from a frequency table.

Starter activity

- Make a frequency table on the whiteboard showing the number of pupils in the class attending morning and afternoon sessions the previous week. If attendance is too good to show much variation either pick a different week or invent a class with variable attendance. Ask pupils to find particular data from the table, e.g. how many attended on Friday morning?

  Ask questions about the data – which is the best/worst day for attendance? Are all the afternoons the same as the mornings? How many more attended on .... than on ....?

Answers to A4/5

1	(a) Tuesday	(b) Friday	(c) 384	(d) 364	(e) 37
	(f) 110				
2	(a) Friday	(b) Wednesday	(c) Tuesday	(d) Friday	(e) Monday
	(f) Friday	(g) Thursday	(h) Wednesday		
	(i) Monday, Tuesday, Wednesday		(j) 202	(k) 932	(l) 807

Unit A4/5 Problems involving interpreting frequency tables

1   A local burger bar has introduced some new products and is keeping a check on the sales.

	Sunday	Monday	Tuesday	Wednesday	Thursday	Friday	Saturday
Fish burger	251	231	198	312	236	562	426
Potato burger	59	71	68	51	82	88	62

(a)   Which day has the least sales? ....

(b)   Which day has the most sales? ....

(c)   What is the difference between the best sales day and the worst? ....

(d)   What is the difference between the best fish burger sales day and the worst?

....

(e)   What is the difference between the best potato burger sales day and the worst?

....

(f)   What is the difference between the worst fish burger sales and the best potato burger sales? ....

2   As part of a road safety project the council is counting traffic passing a school. They count the vehicles passing for one hour before and after school.

		Monday	Tuesday	Wednesday	Thursday	Friday
Morning	**Cars and small vans**	890	705	595	617	691
	Large vans and lorries	194	298	312	215	185
Afternoon	**Cars and small vans**	496	503	421	720	887
	Large vans and lorries	311	295	214	195	106

(a)   Which day is busiest for cars and small vans? ....

(b)   Which day is quietest for cars and small vans? ....

(c)   Which day is busiest for large vans and lorries? ....

(d)   Which day is quietest for large vans and lorries? ....

(e)   Which day has the busiest morning traffic? ....

(f)   Which day has the busiest afternoon traffic? ....

(g)   Which day has the quietest morning traffic? ....

(h)   Which day has the quietest afternoon traffic? ....

(i)   Which mornings have busier traffic than the afternoon? ....

(j)   On Tuesday, how many more cars and small vans were there in the morning than in the afternoon? ....

(k)   How many vehicles did they count on Thursday morning? ....

(l)   How many vehicles did they count on Monday afternoon? ....

Unit A4/6 Problems involving addition of money and decimals

PNS Framework objective

- Solve one-step and two-step problems involving numbers, money or measures, including time; choose and carry out appropriate calculations, using calculator methods where appropriate.

Unit learning outcome

- Problems involving addition of money and decimals.

Prior knowledge

- Knowledge of place value including decimals.
- Able to use vertical addition of numbers with decimals, including money, with exchange.
- Able to use vertical subtraction of money including exchange.

Starter activity

- Make up a short shopping list with typical prices. Decide how much is in the shopper's purse. Add up the cost – *Does the shopper have enough money? If yes how much change, if no what needs to be deleted from the list?* Repeat with a new shopping list and budget.

Answers to A4/6

1	(a) £15.63	(b) £19.32	(c) £13.33	(d) £17.15
	(e) £17.47	(f) £16.84	(g) £21.45	(h) £19.80
2	(a) 67 548.2	(b) 67 552.1	(c) 67 557.6	(d) 67 565.0
	(e) 67 568.8	(f) 67 573.0	(g) 67 574.6	(h) 67 574.9

Unit A4/6 Problems involving addition of money and decimals

1   It's just a few days before Christmas and Bernard the turkey has escaped with just
£22.37 saved up.
He needs a disguise and finds a fancy dress shop.
He finds a fancy dress shop and sees these prices:

dark glasses	£2.95	firefighter's helmet	£2.50
false beard	£2.49	stocking mask	£3.37
blonde wig	£4.15	traffic warden's uniform	£12.68
cowboy outfit	£10.83	wedding dress	£14.35

He tries on the following. Find the cost and how much change he would have.

(a)   Traffic warden's uniform with dark glasses.   Cost .... Change ....

(b)   Traffic warden's uniform with blonde wig   Cost .... Change ....
and false beard.

(c)   Cowboy outfit and firefighter's helmet.   Cost .... Change ....

(d)   Cowboy outfit, dark glasses and stocking   Cost .... Change ....
mask.

(e)   Cowboy outfit, blonde wig and false beard.   Cost .... Change ....

(f)   Wedding dress and false beard.   Cost .... Change ....

(g)   Wedding dress, blonde wig and dark glasses.   Cost .... Change ....

(h)   Wedding dress, firefighter's helmet and   Cost .... Change ....
dark glasses.

2   Father Christmas uses a Land Rover to drive around when the reindeer have a day off.
He keeps a record of the distance he drives so that he can claim back the petrol tax.
When he left the house on 23rd December the milometer read 0 6 7 5 4 2 6

What will it read when he has driven:

(a)   5.6 miles to the newsagents?

(b)   3.9 miles from the newsagents to the supermarket?

(c)   5.5 miles from the supermarket to the toy factory?

(d)   7.4 miles from the factory to the pub?

(e)   3.8 miles from the pub to the warehouse?

(f)   4.2 miles from the warehouse to the sweetshop?

(g)   1.6 miles from the sweetshop to the stables?

(h)   0.3 miles from the stables back to his house?

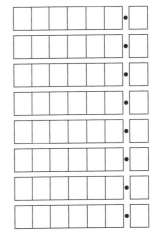

Unit A4/7 Problems involving division with remainders

PNS Framework objectives

- Solve one-step and two-step problems involving numbers, money or measures, including time; choose and carry out appropriate calculations, using calculator methods where appropriate.
- Develop and use written methods to record, support and explain multiplication and division of two-digit numbers by a one-digit number, including division with remainders (e.g. 15 × 9, 98 ÷ 6).

Unit learning outcome

- Problems involving division with remainders.

Prior knowledge

- Competent at times tables up to 10 × 10.
- Able to carry out division with remainders.

Starter activities

- Play the 'Division race'.

  How to play: Pupils sit in groups around a table, with 50 cubes (or other sorting objects) in the centre. You call out a number which the cubes must be sorted into. The first group to sort them into sets and declare how many sets and how many remaining wins a point. After a few tries, increase the number of cubes each group has.

- Play 'Join Up 1' (as per *Jumpstart! Numeracy*, John Taylor, David Fulton Publishers).

Answers to A4/7

1 (a) 33 boxes, 1 cake left over (b) 25 boxes, none left over (c) 20 boxes, none left over
  (d) 16 boxes, 4 cakes left over (e) 14 boxes, 2 cakes left over (f) 12 boxes, 4 cakes left over
  (g) 1 box, 1 cake left over (h) 10 boxes, none left over

2 (a) 4 boxes of slippers and 12 slippers left over (b) 21 pairs (c) 5
  (d) 33 can wear one on each head (one hat left over)
  (e) 15 taxis (with three seats to spare)

3 Monday £5.86 each and 13p added onto the next day's total
  Tuesday £9.30 each and 2p added onto the next day's total
  Wednesday £12.37 each and 1p added onto the next day's total
  Thursday £10.53 each and 2p added onto the next day's total
  Friday £14.60 each and 1p added onto the next day's total
  Saturday £31.13 each exactly, no remainder

Unit A4/7 Problems involving division with remainders

1   A baker has 100 cakes to pack into boxes. He doesn't want any cakes left over. He tried:

(a)   3 in a box.   There would be .... boxes of 3 and .... cakes left over.

(b)   4 in a box.   There would be .... boxes of 4 and .... cakes left over.

(c)   5 in a box.   There would be .... boxes of 5 and .... cakes left over.

(d)   6 in a box.   There would be .... boxes of 6 and .... cakes left over.

(e)   7 in a box.   There would be .... boxes of 7 and .... cakes left over.

(f)   8 in a box.   There would be .... boxes of 8 and .... cakes left over.

(g)   9 in a box.   There would be .... boxes of 9 and .... cakes left over.

(h)   10 in a box.   There would be .... boxes of 10 and .... cakes left over.

2   A spaceship-load of aliens have come to Earth to do their Christmas shopping.

(a)   They have 7 identical feet each.

How many boxes of 24 slippers would 12 aliens need to buy? ....

There would be .... spare slippers left over.

(b)   How many pairs of socks would 6 aliens need? ....

(c)   For dinner 9 aliens shared a box of 50 spanners.

How many got an extra spanner? ....

(d)   They buy a box of 100 cheap woolly hats from the market.

How many aliens can wear one on each of its three heads? ....

Monday	£23.47
Tuesday	£37.19
Wednesday	£49.47
Thursday	£42.13
Friday	£58.39
Saturday	£124.51

(f)   How many 6-seater taxis would they need for all 87 to get back to their spaceship? ....

3   A group of four street entertainers share each day's takings equally.

If they have a remainder they add it onto the next day's total.

How much did they take home each day?

Monday   .... each and .... left over for the next day.

Tuesday   .... each and .... left over for the next day.

Wednesday .... each and .... left over for the next day.

Thursday   .... each and .... left over for the next day.

Friday .... each and .... left over for the next day.

Saturday   .... each and .... left over for the next day.

Unit A4/8 Problems involving multiplication

PNS Framework objectives

- Solve one-step and two-step problems involving numbers, money or measures, including time; choose and carry out appropriate calculations, using calculator methods where appropriate.
- Develop and use written methods to record, support and explain multiplication and division of two-digit numbers by a one-digit number, including division with remainders (e.g. 15×9, $98 \div 6$).

Unit learning outcome

- Problems involving multiplication.

Prior knowledge

- Competent at times tables up to 10×10.
- Able to carry out vertical multiplication with exchange.
- Able to halve three-digit numbers.

Starter activity

- Practise using multiplication shortcuts such as:
    - To multiply a number by 4, double it and double again
    - To multiply by 5, multiply by 10 by adding a zero and halve the answer
    - To multiply by 20, multiply by 10 by adding a zero and double the answer
    - To multiply a number by 19, multiply by 20 then subtract the original number
    Who can use these tricks in their head?

Answers to A4/8

1	(a) 150	(b) 140	(c) 180	(d) 38	(e) 48
	(f) 32	(g) 72	(h) 42	(i) 96	(j) 96
2	(a) $28 \times 3 = 84$	(b) $28 \times 4 = 112$	(c) $26 \times 4 = 104$	(d) $26 \times 3 = 78$
3	(a) 300 books	(b) 550 books	(c) 450 books	(d) 375 books
4	(a) 1200 pencils	(b) 54 rolls of tape	(c) 950 pens	(d) 48 rulers

---

Unit A4/8 Problems involving multiplication

A school is ordering stock for next year.

1   How many will they get if they buy:
    (a)   75 packs containing 2 rolls of sticky tape? ....
    (b)   14 packs of 10 AA batteries? ....
    (c)   36 packs of 5 'C' whiteboard marker pens? ....
    (d)   19 packs of 2 calculator batteries? ....
    (e)   8 packs of 6 pencil sharpeners? ....
    (f)   4 packs of 8 pairs of scissors ....
    (g)   9 packs of 8 red crayons? ....
    (h)   7 packs of 6 blue crayons? ....
    (i)   8 packs of 12 'jumbo' pencils? ....
    (j)   6 packs of 16 folders? ....

2   They expect each Year 4 child to use 3 English books and 4 Maths books in a year.
    (a)   How many English books will a class of 13 boys and 15 girls need? ....
    (b)   How many Maths books will the same Year 4 class need? ....
    (c)   The other Year 4 class has 14 boys and 12 girls. How many Maths books do they
           need? ....
    (d)   How many English books does this other class need? ....

3   Last year they ordered too many of some books so they are halving this year's order.
    (a)   Last year they bought 600 History books, so this year they will buy ....
    (b)   Last year they bought 1100 Science books, so this year they will buy ....
    (c)   Last year they bought 900 Geography books, so this year they will buy ....
    (d)   Last year they bought 750 word books, so this year they will buy ....

4   Last year they ran out of some things. How many will they buy if:
    (a)   They double last year's order for 600 pencils? ....
    (b)   They triple last year's order for 18 rolls of sticky tape? ....
    (c)   They double last year's order for 475 handwriting pens? ....
    (d)   They triple last year's order for 16 rulers? ....

Unit A4/9 Problems involving multiplication and division of money

PNS Framework objective

- Solve one-step and two-step problems involving numbers, money or measures, including time; choose and carry out appropriate calculations, using calculator methods where appropriate.

Unit learning outcome

- Problems involving multiplication and division of money.

Prior knowledge

- Competent at times tables up to 10×10.
- Able to carry out vertical multiplication with exchange.
- Able to halve three-digit numbers.

Starter activity

- Practise using multiplication shortcuts such as:
  Moving columns (or the decimal point) to multiply/divide by 10 or 100 – use a place value multiplier as illustrated in M3/2

  To multiply a number by 4, double it and double again
  To multiply a number by 8, double it and double again and double a third time
  To divide a whole number by 10 insert a decimal point to the left of the units digit.

Answers to A4/9

1	(a) £2.80	(b) £2.60	(c) £5.00	(d) £288	(e) £213
	(f) £96	(g) £20.80	(h) £7.60	(i) £3.60	(j) £30
2	(a) 20p	(b) 20p	(c) £12.50	(d) £27	
3	(a) 24 disks	(b) 14 books	(c) 25 rubbers	(d) 28 with £1 left over	
4	(a) £2.40	(b) £1.20	(c) £5.50	(d) £1.75	

Unit A4/9 Problems involving multiplication and division of money

Work out the answers to these and just write down the answers. See how many you can work out in your head.

1   Find the cost of:
   (a)   28 pencils costing 10p each. ....
   (b)   4 whiteboard pens at 65p each. ....
   (c)   125 sheets of card at 4p each. ....
   (d)   72 books at £4 each. ....
   (e)   6 computer CD-ROMs at £35.50 each. ....
   (f)   32 dictionaries costing £3 each. ....
   (g)   8 fountain pens at £2.60 each. ....
   (h)   95 cheap pencil sharpeners at 8p each. ....
   (i)   8 good pencil sharpeners at 45p each. ....
   (j)   8 packs of A4 paper at £3.75 each. ....

2   How much does one cost if you buy:
   (a)   50 rulers for £10? ....
   (b)   12 roller-ball pens for £2.40? ....
   (c)   8 atlases for £100? ....
   (d)   4 globes for £108? ....

3   (a)   How many 8p floppy disks can you buy for £1.92? ....
   (b)   How many £2.50 reading books can you buy for £35? ....
   (c)   How many 9p rubbers can you buy for £2.25? ....
   (d)   How many £1.25 marker pens can you buy for £36? ....

4   (a)   If 100 sheets of backing paper cost £24, how much do 10 sheets cost? ....
   (b)   If 60 crayons cost £7.20, how much do 10 crayons cost? ....
   (c)   If 4 storage boxes cost £22, how much does 1 box cost? ....
   (d)   If 8 sets of felt pens cost £14, how much does 1 set cost? ....

Unit A4/10 Problems involving multiplication and division

PNS Framework objectives

- Solve one-step and two-step problems involving numbers, money or measures, including time; choose and carry out appropriate calculations, using calculator methods where appropriate.
- Use a calculator to carry out one-step and two-step calculations involving all four operations; recognise negative numbers in the display, correct mistaken entries and interpret the display correctly in the context of money.

Unit learning outcome

- Problems involving multiplication and division.

Prior knowledge

- Competent at times tables up to 10×10.
- Able to carry out vertical multiplication of TUs with exchange.
- Able to divide HTUs with exchange.

Starter activity

- Discuss what the class would need if catering for their own class party – what items to buy. Work out how many of each item would be needed by multiplying how many each child might have by the number of children in the class.

  Discuss what size of multipacks different items *might* come in, 10s, 24s, 48s – how many multipacks would have to be bought, what would be left over (as per sheet A4/7)?

Answers to A4/10

Year 3 have: 240 plain biscuits, 240 custard creams, 72 bags of crisps
Each child will get: 10 plain biscuits, 10 custard creams, 3 bags of crisps
Year 4 have: 84 marshmallow biscuits, 140 choc ices, 168 ginger biscuits
Each child will get: 3 marshmallow biscuits, 5 choc ices, 6 ginger biscuits, 8 peanuts
Year 5 have: 100 sausage rolls, 100 cans of pop
Each child will get: 4 sausage rolls, 4 cans of pop
Year 6 have: 156 ice lollies, 182 cheese and pineapple on a stick, 208 cheese rolls
Each child will get: 6 ice lollies, 7 cheese and pineapple on a stick, 8 cheese rolls

Unit A4/10 Problems involving multiplication and division

This year the school Christmas party was a bit of a disaster. The children had been asked to bring party food. No one organised who should bring what.

Here is what each year group had.

Use multiplication to find out how much each year group had of each item.

Use division to share it out among the children in that year group.

Year 3 (24 children) had:
8 packets of 30 plain biscuits
10 packets of custard cream biscuits
12 bags each containing 6 packets of crisps
Altogether they had .... plain biscuits
.... custard creams
.... packets of crisps

When shared out each child will get
....
....
....

Year 4 (28 children) had:
7 packets of 12 marshmallow biscuits
14 packets of 10 choc ices
6 packets of 28 ginger biscuits
1 bag containing 224 peanuts (yes they really did have to count them!)
Altogether they had .... marshmallow
biscuits
.... choc ices
.... ginger biscuits
224 peanuts
When shared out each child will get
....
....

Year 5 (25 children) had:
3 margarine tubs, each containing 20 sausage rolls
1 tin containing another 40 sausage rolls
4 packs of 24 cans of pop
4 loose cans of pop
Altogether they had .... sausage rolls
.... cans of pop

When shared out each child will get
....
....
....

Year 6 (26 children) had:
13 packets of 12 ice lollies
7 boxes containing 26 cheese and pineapple on a stick
13 packets of 12 ice lollies
8 plates of 9 cheese rolls
4 plates of 10 cheese rolls
8 plates of 12 cheese rolls
Altogether they had .... ice lollies
.... sticks with
cheese and pineapple
.... cheese rolls
When shared out each child will get
....
....

Unit A4/11 Making and interpreting Venn diagrams and bar graphs

PNS Framework objective

- Represent a puzzle or problem using number sentences, statements or diagrams; use these to solve the problem; present and interpret the solution in the context of the problem.

Unit learning outcome

- Making and interpreting Venn diagrams and bar graphs.

Prior knowledge

- This unit follows and reinforces work from Units D4/2 and 3.
- Understands sets and Venn diagrams.
- Able to use a ruler accurately to draw bar graph columns.

Starter activity

- Draw a Venn diagram on the whiteboard with three criteria: 'have a brother or sister in this school', 'have a brother or sister in a different school' and 'have a brother or sister not in any school' (too young or too old). Discuss the properties of each sector and make labels (e.g. 'has a brother or sister in this school and in another school') to place on tables. Ask children to sit at the table that matches them. Go around each table and check, asking those on the correct table to add their name in the correct sector of the diagram on the whiteboard.

Answers to A4/11

1

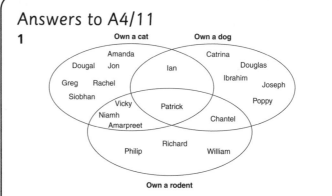

2
(a) Amanda, Dougal, Jon, Greg, Rachel, Siobhan
(b) Catrina, Douglas, Ibrahim, Joseph, Poppy
(c) Philip, Richard, William   (d) Ian
(e) Chantel   (f) Amarpreet, Niamh, Vicky
(g) Patrick

3

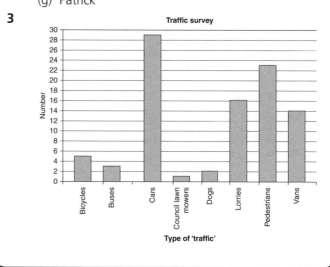

Unit A4/11 Making and interpreting Venn diagrams and bar graphs

1   Some of these children own more than one pet. Put their names in the Venn diagram to show what pets they own.

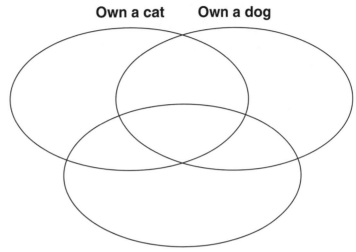

Cat owners
Amanda, Amarpreet, Dougal, Ian, Greg, Jon, Niamh, Patrick, Rachel, Siobhan and Vicky

Dog owners
Catrina, Chantel, Douglas, Ian, Ibrahim, Joseph, Patrick and Poppy

Rodent owners (hamster, mouse, rat, gerbil)
Amarpreet, Chantel, Niamh, Patrick, Philip, Richard, Vicky and William

2   Which children own:

(a)   only cats? ....

(b)   only dogs? ....

(c)   only rodents? ....

(d)   dogs and cats? ....

(e)   dogs and rodents? ....

(f)   cats and rodents? ....

(g)   cats, dogs and rodents? ....

3   Use this data to complete the bar graph.

'Traffic' passing in 30 minutes

bicycles	5
buses	3
cars	29
council lawn mowers	1
dogs	2
lorries	16
pedestrians	23
vans	14

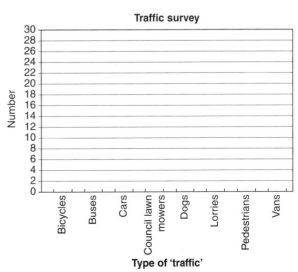

Unit A4/12 Problems with perimeter, area and mass

PNS Framework objectives

- Represent a puzzle or problem using number sentences, statements or diagrams; use these to solve the problem; present and interpret the solution in the context of the problem.
- Draw rectangles and measure and calculate their perimeters; find the area of rectilinear shapes drawn on a square grid by counting squares.

Unit learning outcome

- Solve problems with perimeter, area and mass.

Prior knowledge

- This unit follows and reinforces work from Units M4/2 and 5.
- Understanding of perimeter and area.
- Familiar with units of mass and volume.
- Able to subtract ThHTUs with exchange.

Starter activity

- Use pinboards and rubber bands to make rectangles of differing areas. Point out that one length and one width is halfway around the shape, half of its perimeter. Work out the perimeter of each rectangle by adding together one width and one length then doubling it.

  Ask children to make a rectangle with a perimeter of 24 squares – advise them that if they halve 24 to make 12, they can then choose two numbers that add up to 12 as the length and width of their rectangle.

Answers to A4/12

1 (a) and (b) Any of four of the following rectangles:

$17 \, m \times 1 \, m = $ area of $17 \, m^2$
$16 \, m \times 2 \, m = $ area of $32 \, m^2$
$15 \, m \times 3 \, m = $ area of $45 \, m^2$
$14 \, m \times 4 \, m = $ area of $56 \, m^2$
$13 \, m \times 5 \, m = $ area of $65 \, m^2$
$12 \, m \times 6 \, m = $ area of $72 \, m^2$
$11 \, m \times 7 \, m = $ area of $77 \, m^2$
$10 \, m \times 8 \, m = $ area of $80 \, m^2$
$9 \, m \times 9 \, m = $ area of $81 \, m^2$

(c) to (e) Various answers depending upon which of the above have been chosen

2 (a) 37.962 kg or 37 962 g   (b) 24.975 kg or 24 975 g

3 (a) 2500 g or 2.5 kg   (b) 4 litres

4 (a) 1000 g or 1 kg   (b) 20 litres

Unit A4/12 Problems with perimeter, area and mass

1   Caroline and Tom are going to make a pen for their chickens. They have four posts and 36 metres of wire mesh.

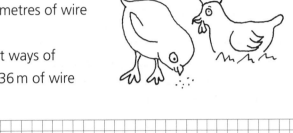

(a)   On the grid, design four different ways of making a rectangular pen using 36 m of wire mesh.

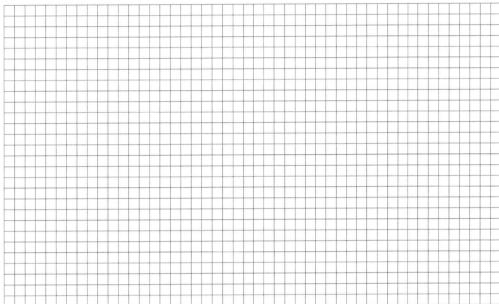

(b)   Work out the area of each of your designs.
Design 1 is .... m long and .... m wide. It has an area of .... m².
Design 2 is .... m long and .... m wide. It has an area of .... m².
Design 3 is .... m long and .... m wide. It has an area of .... m².
Design 4 is .... m long and .... m wide. It has an area of .... m².

(c)   Which of your designs has the smallest area? ....

(d)   Which of your designs has the largest area? ....

(e)   What is the difference between the largest and smallest? .... m².

2   The school cook has ordered supplies but put down **g** instead of **kg**.

(a)   She needed 38 kg of sugar but only got 38 g. How much more is needed? ....

(b)   She wanted 25 kg of flour but only got 25 g. How much more is needed? ....

3   The cook is using instant custard. The instructions say mix 250 g in 1 litre of boiling water.

(a)   How much mixture is needed for 10 litres of water? ....

(b)   How much water is needed for 1 kg of mixture? ....

4   She decides to make it thinner by adding only 200 g to a litre of water.

(a)   How much mixture does she mix with 10 litres of water? ....

(b)   How much water does she add to 4 kg of mixture? ....

Unit A4/13 Problems with time intervals

PNS Framework objectives

- Represent a puzzle or problem using number sentences, statements or diagrams; use these to solve the problem; present and interpret the solution in the context of the problem.
- Read time to the nearest minute; use a.m., p.m. and 12-hour clock notation; choose units of time to measure time intervals; calculate time intervals from clocks and timetables.

Unit learning outcome

- To solve problems with time intervals.

Prior knowledge

- This unit follows and reinforces work from Units M4/6 and 7.
- Able to read and interpret times expressed in 24-hour, four-digit format.

Starter activity

- Use the counting-on method to work out some familiar time intervals, e.g. duration of morning school, school day, etc., for example:

10 mins + 1 hour + 35 mins   1 hour + 35 mins + 10 mins = **1 hour 45 mins**

08:50   09:00   10:00   **10:35**

Introduce a simple method of finding time intervals by subtraction, for example:

9	60	
~~10~~	35	1 Exchange 1 hour for 60 minutes
08	50	2 Subtract 50 from the 60 minutes then add on the 35 minutes

Try both methods, do children have a preference?

Answers to A4/13

1 (a) 5 hours 35 mins   (b) 6 hours 13 mins   (c) 5 hours 18 mins
(d) 5 hours 3 mins
2 (a) 1 hour 55 mins   (b) 1 hour 42 mins   (c) 1 hour 42 mins
(d) 1 hour 24 mins
3 Choice of answer, but (a) best choice is option 4, (b) because it has the shortest time waiting at coach and bus stops

Unit A4/13 Problems with time intervals

Just before Christmas Day last year, Bernard the turkey noticed that a lot of his friends at the turkey farm seemed to disappear. He only discovered what had happened when he found an old cookery book by the dustbins. Bernard has been planning his escape for several months, looking carefully at bus and coach timetables. He has phoned the 'Poultry Palace' animal sanctuary in Devon. They've sent him a disguise and his bus fares.

Bernard has four options.

He has to be careful not to spend too long standing around waiting for buses in case he is recognised.

Look closely at his four options.

	Option 1	Option 2	Option 3	Option 4
Escape from turkey farm	06:25	07:30	09:45	11:15
Catch bus from village	06:30	07:35	09:53	11:20
Arrive in Birmingham	08:55	10:25	12:18	13:55
Leave Birmingham on coach	09:40	11:40	12:40	14:10
Arrive in Bristol	11:15	13:28	14:08	14:46
Leave Bristol on bus	12:20	13:50	15:20	15:50
Arrive at animal sanctuary	13:55	15:25	16:45	17:42

1   How long will be spent travelling if he takes:
   (a)   Option 1? ....
   (b)   Option 2? ....
   (c)   Option 3? ....
   (d)   Option 4? ....
2   How long will be spent waiting if he takes:
   (a)   Option 1? ....
   (b)   Option 2? ....
   (c)   Option 3? ....
   (d)   Option 4? ....
3   (a)   If you were Bernard which option would you choose? ....
   (b)   Give reasons for your choice. ....

Unit A4/14 Problems with shape and co-ordinates

PNS Framework objective

*   Draw polygons and classify them by identifying their properties, including their line symmetry.

Unit learning outcome

*   Solve problems with shape and co-ordinates.

Prior knowledge

*   This unit follows and reinforces work from Units S4/1 and 4.
*   Knowledge of names and properties of polygons.
*   Able to identify co-ordinates.

Starter activities

*   'Shape Snap'. Have ready a set of large 'snap' cards showing polygons including: isosceles triangle, right-angled isosceles triangle, right-angled non-isosceles, pentagon, hexagon, octagon, oblong and square. Half of the cards should have shapes drawn on them, the others just the name of the shape, e.g. 'right-angled triangle', 'isosceles triangle', 'equilateral triangle'. Mix all the cards together and divide into two playing piles for two halves of the class. Allow children to 'snap' two cards if they have matching criteria, e.g. both are isosceles though one is right-angled, or both are right-angled though only one is isosceles.
*   Quickly revise which way round co-ordinates are given, using a helpful phrase such as 'In through the front door then up the stairs' to remind them to look along the x-axis before going up the y-axis.

Answers to A4/14

Children should have drawn the following shapes but the co-ordinates of the corners will vary according to where they have chosen to place them on the grid:

(a)   an isosceles triangle
(b)   a hexagon
(c)   an octagon
(d)   an oblong that is twice as long as it is wide
(e)   a right-angled triangle that is also isosceles
(f)   a right-angled triangle that is not isosceles
(g)   an irregular polygon of their own design.

Unit A4/14 Problems with shape and co-ordinates

1   Draw the following shapes on the grid below and write down the co-ordinates of the corners. Label them (a) to (g).

Example: the oblong drawn already on the grid has corners at (1, 11), (1, 14), (3, 14) and (3, 11)

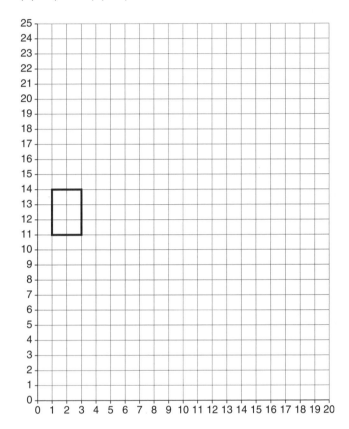

(a)   an isosceles triangle (........., ...), (........., ...), (........., ...)

(b)   a hexagon (........., ...), (........., ...), (........., ...), (........., ...), (........., ...), (........., ...)

(c)   an octagon (........., ...), (........., ...), (........., ...), (........., ...), (........., ...), (........., ...)

(d)   an oblong that is twice as long as it is wide (........., ...), (........., ...), (........., ...), (........., ...)

(e)   a right-angled triangle that is also isosceles (........., ...), (........., ...), (........., ...)

(f)   a right-angled triangle that is not isosceles (........., ...), (........., ...), (........., ...)

(g)   an irregular polygon of your own design (........., ...), (........., ...), (........., ...)

Unit S3/1 2-D shapes

PNS Framework objective

- Relate 2-D shapes and 3-D solids to drawings of them; describe, visualise, classify, draw and make the shapes.

Unit learning outcome

- To use mathematical criteria to classify and describe 2-D shapes.

Prior knowledge

- Understands that regular 2-D shapes are flat.
- Is familiar with terms such as straight, edge, angle, right angle.
- Can compare the lengths of sides.

Starter activity

- Play 'Shape Snap' with the class split into several teams – each 'snap' wins a point, false alarms lose a point. You can use commercially produced cards or have the children make a set using shape templates and uniform-sized pieces of card.

  Use a shape recognition computer program or maths game website.

Answers to S3/1

1 A: rectangle (or oblong) with four right angles and two pairs of equal sides

B: square with four right angles and four equal sides

C: octagon, eight equal sides

D: hexagon, six equal sides

E: (right-angled) triangle, three sides

F: pentagon with two right angles and five sides

G: (quadrilateral) parallelogram, no right angles, two pairs of equal sides

H: rectangle (or oblong) with four right angles and two pairs of equal sides

I: triangle, no right angle, three sides

J: pentagon, no right angles, five sides

K: rectangle (or oblong) with four right angles and two pairs of equal sides

L: quadrilateral, no right angles, no equal sides

2 Answers will vary

3 (a) 2   (b) 1

Unit S3/1 2-D shapes

This page is about 2-D shapes, that means shapes that are flat and only have two dimensions, width and length.

If a shape has three straight sides and three angles it must be a triangle. Some triangles have a right angle, some have two or three sides the same length.

If a shape has four straight sides it is called a quadrilateral.

A *rectangle* has four straight sides and four right angles. Each side is the same length as a side opposite.

An *oblong* is a rectangle with two pairs of equal sides.

A *square* is a special sort of rectangle because it has all four sides the same length.

Other straight-sided shapes include: **pentagon** – five sides, **hexagon** – six sides, **octagon** – eight sides.

1   Write down the name of each shape below and describe it.
    Example: This is a square because it has four equal sides and four right angles.

A ....
B ....
C ....
D ....
E ....
F ....
G ....
H ....
I ....
J ....
K ....
L ....

2   Using squared paper, draw and label these shapes:
    (a)   a quadrilateral with no right angles.
    (b)   a pentagon with three right angles.
    (c)   a triangle with a right angle and two sides the same length.
    (d)   a semi-circle.
    (e)   a triangle with all three sides different lengths.
    (f)   a circle.

3   How many sides does:
    (a)   the semi-circle have? ....   (b)   the circle have? ....

Challenge

Draw a rectangle and divide it up into smaller, straight-edged shapes. Cut them out carefully. Now sort them out into sets of triangles, quadrilaterals and so on. Can you put them back together to make a rectangle again?

Unit S3/2 3-D shapes

PNS Framework objective

- Relate 2-D shapes and 3-D solids to drawings of them; describe, visualise, classify, draw and make the shapes.

Unit learning outcome

- To use mathematical criteria to classify and describe 3-D shapes.

Prior knowledge

- Understands that regular 3-D shapes are 3-dimensional and 'solid'.
- Is familiar with terms such as triangular, circular, rectangular and curved.

Starter activities

- Examine a variety of regular solid shapes – books, boxes, pencil cases, etc. Sort them according to different criteria: 'has/does not have curved face', 'has/does not have square face', 'will/won't roll'.
- Carefully open out cartons (from breakfast cereals, chocolate boxes, etc.) to reveal the nets from which they were made.

Answers to S3/2

1   A: square-based pyramid, one square and four triangular faces
    B: cube, six square faces
    C: triangular prism, two triangular and three rectangular faces
    D: cuboid, six rectangular (or oblong) faces
    E: cylinder, two circular faces and one curved
    F: sphere, one curved face.

Unit S3/2 3-D shapes

This page is about 3-D shapes, that means shapes that are solid.

They have **3** Dimensions – height, width and length.

Each surface of a solid shape is called a *face*.

If a solid is the same shape and size all the way through we call it a prism.

If it is the same shape all the way through but narrows to a point it is a pyramid.

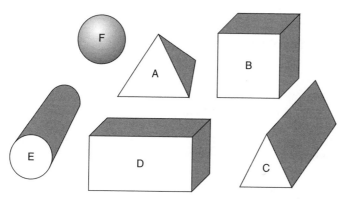

1   Name the solid shapes.

2   Describe each shape to explain how you know it is what you say it is. Example: This is a cube because all six faces are square.

	Name of shape	Description of shape
A	....	....
B	....	....
C	....	....
D	....	....
E	....	....
F	....	....

Challenge

Using squared paper draw out the 'net' of one of these 'solid' shapes.

If you get it right you should be able to cut it out and fold it up into the solid shape you designed it to be.

Unit S3/3 Symmetry and reflections, 3-D shapes

PNS Framework objective

- Draw and complete shapes with reflective symmetry; draw the reflection of a shape in a mirror line along one side.

Unit learning outcome

- To identify lines of symmetry and reflections.

Prior knowledge

- Familiar with the concept of line symmetry.
- Knows and can correctly use the term 'line of symmetry'.

Starter activity

- Fold paper and cut out a random shape, starting on the fold and ending further along the fold. Open out to see the complete, symmetrical shape.

  Challenge the pupils to use this method to make one of the following without drawing guide lines on the paper:

  - a teddy bear shape   – a male or female toilet door symbol
  - a house shape   – a Christmas tree.

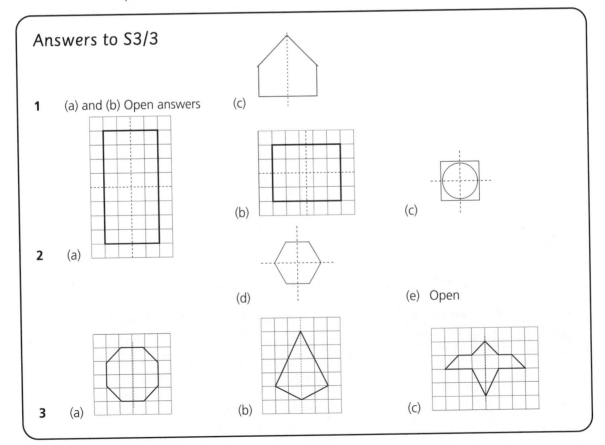

Answers to S3/3

1   (a) and (b) Open answers   (c)

2   (a)

    (b)   (c)

    (d)   (e) Open

3   (a)   (b)   (c)

Unit S3/3 Symmetry and reflections, 3-D shapes

You need squared paper to do questions 1 and 2.

1   Draw these objects on squared paper and draw one line of symmetry like this:

   (a)   One of your classroom windows.

   (b)   A cupboard or a classroom door.

   (c)   This shape:

2   Draw these shapes and put in two lines of symmetry like this:

   (a)   An oblong eight squares tall and four squares wide.

   (b)   An oblong four squares tall and five squares wide.

   (c)   A square with a circle inside it.

   (d)   A hexagon.

   (e)   A shape of your own.

3   Here are some half pictures. Draw in the line of symmetry, copy the half that is shown here, then add on the missing half.

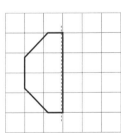

(a)

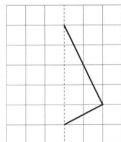

(b)

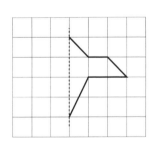

(c)

Challenge

Draw a house front which is symmetrical, and where every feature is also symmetrical.

Unit S3/4 Position and movement

PNS Framework objective

- Read and record the vocabulary of position, direction and movement, using the four compass directions to describe movement about a grid.

Unit learning outcome

- To use the vocabulary of position and movement.

Prior knowledge

- Able to draw short lines of specified length.
- Able to use four-point compass directions.
- Able to use 'clockwise' and 'anti-clockwise'.

Starter activity

- Play 'Remote control' – the object is to guide a pupil around the room using verbal instructions.

  Label the walls with compass points North, South, East and West. The volunteer is put in a starting position, and an intended stopping position is identified without them seeing. Pupils take it in turns to give an instruction by specifying a direction and a number of steps.

  The pupil who gives the final, successful instruction swaps places with the volunteer and is then guided to a new position in the classroom.

Answers to S3/4

1 Open answers

2 (a) 5
  (b) 2
  (c) Cheese and onion
  (d) Salt and vinegar

3

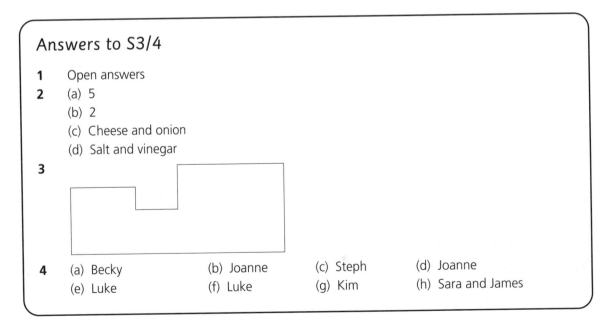

4 (a) Becky   (b) Joanne   (c) Steph   (d) Joanne
  (e) Luke   (f) Luke   (g) Kim   (h) Sara and James

Unit S3/4 Position and movement

1 (a) Number these stairs in **ascending** order (going up)

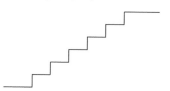

(b) Number these stairs in **descending** order (going down)

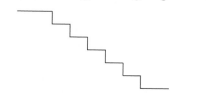

S3/4

2 A shop stacks its boxes of crisps like this.
Each flavour is in a different column.

(a) How many columns are there? ....

(b) How many complete rows are there? ....

(c) Which column has most boxes? ....

(d) Which is the shortest column? ....

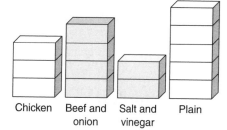

Chicken   Beef and   Salt and   Plain
           onion   vinegar

3 Here is the route taken by a robot. It started from the + in the centre of the rectangle.
Use straight lines to draw its route using these directions:

(a) Go North for 2 cm

(b) Go East 5 cm

(c) Go South 4 cm

(d) Go West for 10 cm

(e) Go North for 3 cm

(f) Go East 3 cm

(g) Go South 1 cm

(h) Go East 2 cm

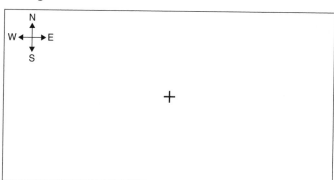

4 Ten children are standing in a circle.

(a) Who is the fifth person from Kim going clockwise? ....

(b) Who is the third from Luke going clockwise? ....

(c) Who is the fourth from Lisa going clockwise? ....

(d) Who is the fourth from Lisa going anti-clockwise? ....

(e) Who is the eighth from Chris going clockwise? ....

(f) Who is the second from Chris going anti-clockwise? ....

(g) Who is standing opposite Becky? ....

(h) Which two people is Lisa standing between? ....

Kim

Joanne   Dan

Chris   Sara

Steph   Lisa

Luke   James

Becky

Challenge

Draw a simple plan of your route to school.

Draw a plan of your table, marking where everything is at the moment.

Unit S3/5 Right angles and half right angles

PNS Framework objective

- Use a set-square to draw right angles and to identify right angles in 2-D shapes; compare angles with a right angle; recognise that a straight line is equivalent to two right angles.

Unit learning outcome

- To make and describe right-angle turns and part right-angle turns.

Prior knowledge

- Understands that the term 'angle' is used to describe the meeting of two lines or surface.
- Understand that the length of the lines or surfaces do not affect the size of the angle.

Starter activity

- Look for right angles within the structure of the room – doors/windows would not fit if the corners were not the right angle. Take four sheets of paper and fit them together using a corner of each. Fit the right-angled corners of other objects together (e.g. four books).

  Make right angles by folding a piece of paper in half then folding the fold in half. Tear scrap paper into irregular, roughly round shapes and make right angles out of these using the fold-twice method. Use these to test whether other angles in the room are right angles.

Answers to S3/5

1 Various answers
2 (a) activity   (b) East   (c) South   (d) 4   (e) 8
3 Activity
4 Activity

Unit S3/5 Right angles and half right angles

If you look around the room you will see many right angles. Try looking at the corners of windows, doors, walls, ceilings and books.

For many things that we make, a right angle is the right angle for the corners.

When we want to highlight a right angle we put a tiny square in the corner like this:

1   Make a list of ten things in the room that have right angles.

2   (a)   Draw a simple compass rose like the one on the right.
            If you know which direction really is North turn it to face
            North.

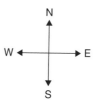

     (b)   Use a pencil as a pointer and place it on your compass rose, facing North.
            Turn the pencil round clockwise through one right angle.
            Which direction is it facing? ....
     (c)   Turn it through another right angle. Where is it facing? ....
     (d)   How many right-angled turns will you need to turn the pencil around one
            complete turn? ....
     (e)   How many half right-angle turns would you need for a complete
            turn? ....

3   (a)   Draw a square and fold it in two diagonally – like this:
     (b)   Cut it in two down the diagonal fold. You should now have triangles, each with
            one right angle and two half right angles.
     (c)   Mark the half right angles.
     (d)   Turn one of the triangles and put them both together to make a larger triangle.
            Keep one half still and turn the other through two right angles.

4   (a)   Make another pair of triangles by cutting a square in half.
     (b)   Mark the half right angles.
     (c)   Tear the half right angles off all four triangles and put them
            together so that the tips are all touching like this:
            Do they fit together? ....

     (d)   Do the four right angles fit together? ....

Challenge

Cut a paper square in half diagonally. Cut one half in half through its right angle.

Now cut one of the halves the same way. Repeat until you have a set of right-angled triangles all different sizes except for the smallest pair.

Now put it back together again!

Unit S4/1 Polygons

PNS Framework objective

- Draw polygons and classify them by identifying their properties, including their line symmetry.

Unit learning outcome

- To classify and describe polygons using mathematical criteria.

Prior knowledge

- Understands that regular 2-D shapes are flat.
- Is familiar with terms such as straight, edge, angle, right angle.
- Can compare the lengths of sides.

Starter activity

- Experiment with making shapes by cutting small pieces of rectangular scrap paper which have been folded in two then open them out, for example:

  - Mark a point on the edges opposite the fold and cut from either end of the fold to the marked point.
  - Do the same but cutting to two points, one either side of the centre of the opposite edge.
  - Fold the paper in two then fold the fold in half. Cut diagonally across from the loose ends of the folded fold to the end of the other fold.

  Use appropriate vocabulary to describe the shapes, comparing the lengths and numbers of sides, are the shapes regular?

Answers to S4/1

1 Oblong
2 Irregular triangle
3 Regular pentagon
4 Regular triangle
5 Regular hexagon
6 Square
7 Regular octagon
8 Irregular pentagon
9 Isosceles triangle
10 Right-angled triangle
11 Equilateral triangle
12 Right-angled isosceles triangle

Unit S4/1 Polygons

Flat, closed shapes with straight edges are all polygons. Their names tell us the number of sides and angles. Here are some words to help:

poly*gon*	means 'many' angles	octa*gon*	means **eight** angles and sides
hexa*gon*	means **six** angles and sides	penta*gon*	means *five* angles and sides
triangle	means **three** angles and sides	deca*gon*	means **ten** angles and sides
hepta*gon*	means **seven** angles and sides	*lateral*	means *side*
*quad*rilateral	means *four* angles and sides	.... *gon*	means *angle*
regular	means that all sides are equal and all angles are equal		
irregular	means that sides are not all equal and angles aren't equal.		

Quadrilaterals with four right angles are also called **rectangles**.

Rectangles with two sides longer than the other two are **oblongs**.

Regular rectangles (with all four sides equal) are better known as **squares**.
Use the words above to write a description of each of these shapes.

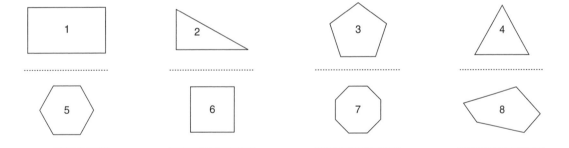

....

....

Use these words to describe the triangles below.

An **equilateral triangle** has equal sides, it is a regular triangle.
An **isosceles triangle** has two sides equal and two angles equal. It has one line of symmetry.
A **right-angled triangle** has one angle that is a right angle – 90°.

....

Challenge

Draw polygons of your own and give them the correct name.

Unit S4/2 3-D shapes

PNS Framework objective

- Visualise 3-D objects from 2-D drawings; make nets of common solids.

Unit learning outcome

- To classify and describe polyhedra using mathematical criteria.

Prior knowledge

- Understands that regular 3-D shapes are three-dimensional and 'solid'.
- Is familiar with names of common 2-D shapes.

Starter activities

- Examine and compare an assortment of plastic solid shapes – look at properties – are they the same shape all the way through?
- Make a prism out of plasticine and carefully slice it into sections. Alternatively, slice up a chocolate bar such as a Milky Way – pieces for those who can name its shape as being either a cuboid or a (rectangular) prism.
- Carefully dismantle card boxes and packets (e.g. boxes from breakfast cereals, tea bags, etc.) and flatten them out to study the nets from which they were made.

Answers to S4/2

Two 'solid' shapes with edges and vertices marked.

Unit S4/2 3-D shapes

Solid shapes which have only flat faces is a polyhedron (more than one are called polyhedra). Each surface is called a *face*.

A *pyramid* has a base from which triangular faces rise up to a point. The shape of the base tells us what sort of pyramid it is.

A *prism* is the same shape all the way through. It gets its name from the shape of the two ends.

Cuboids are prisms with six rectangular faces. Opposite faces are the same as each other.

A *cube* has six square faces.

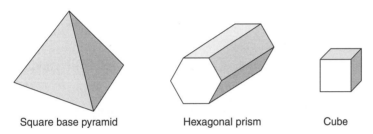

Square base pyramid   Hexagonal prism   Cube

At the bottom of this sheet are the nets of a cuboid and a triangle-based pyramid.

1   Cut them both out carefully, fold along the dotted lines and stick them together.
2   Use a felt pen to mark the *edges* – places where TWO faces meet.
3   Use a different colour felt pen to mark each *vertex* – places where THREE faces meet.

Challenge

Use squared paper and shape templates to make the net of a different prism and pyramid.

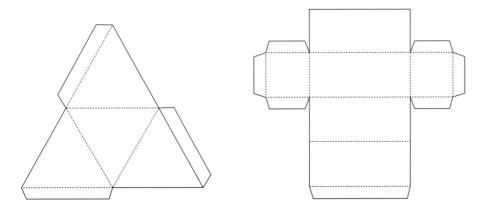

Unit S4/3 Line symmetry

PNS Framework objective

- Draw polygons and classify them by identifying their properties, including their line symmetry.

Unit learning outcome

- To understand and use line symmetry.

Prior knowledge

- Familiar with the concept of line symmetry.
- Knows and can correctly use the term 'line of symmetry'.

Starter activity

- Fold paper and cut out a random shape, starting on the fold and ending further along the fold. Open out to see the complete, symmetrical shape.

  Challenge the pupils to use this method to make one of the following without drawing guide lines on the paper:
  - a teddy bear shape
  - a male or female toilet door symbol
  - a house shape
  - a Christmas tree

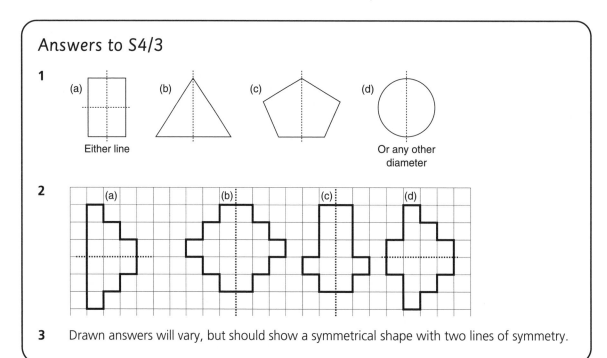

Answers to S4/3

1 (a) Either line (b) (c) (d) Or any other diameter

2 (a) (b) (c) (d)

3 Drawn answers will vary, but should show a symmetrical shape with two lines of symmetry.

Unit S4/3 Line symmetry

If a shape can be folded exactly in half we say it is *symmetrical*.

The line of the fold is called **the axis of symmetry**. If you place a mirror down the line of symmetry the shape will look complete.

Some shapes have more than one line of symmetry.

S4/3

1   Draw one line of symmetry on the shapes below.

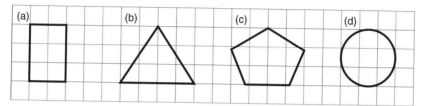

2   Shapes do not have to be regular to be symmetrical.
     Draw the missing halves to these symmetrical shapes.

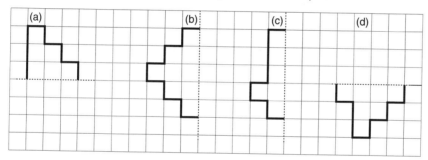

3   Draw a shape that has more than one line of symmetry.

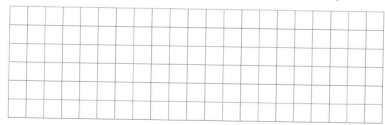

Challenge

Draw the following and mark on the axis of symmetry: a teddy bear, a doll, the front of a car, a face.

Unit S4/4 Co-ordinates

PNS Framework objective

- Recognise horizontal and vertical lines; use the eight compass points to describe direction; describe and identify the position of a square on a grid of squares.

Unit learning outcome

- To read co-ordinates in the first quadrant.

Prior knowledge

- Able to read values from horizontal and vertical scales.

Starter activity

- Ideally this activity should be done in an uncluttered open area such as the school hall or playground.

  Mark a position in the bottom left-hand corner of the area as the 'Start', where the imaginary x-axis and y-axis meet. Place an object in the main area (the first quadrant).

  One child walks along each axis counting steps until they draw level with the object, thus establishing the co-ordinates.

  Place a second object on the floor and ask children to predict the co-ordinates based on the first object – is it closer to the start or further away? Find out the position by walking along the axes.

Answers to S4/4

1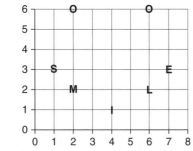

2 (a) (8,6) (b) (6,2) (c) (2,4) (d) (2,6) (e) (5,4)
(f) (6,3) (g) (7,7) (h) (3,2)

3 Answers will vary, should decide the location of the swimming baths and a petrol station, mark them on the map and record the co-ordinates of both.

Unit S4/4 Co-ordinates

We can mark positions on a grid using **co-ordinates**.
This is very useful for finding and recording places on maps.

Co-ordinates are a pair of numbers that give the position of something on the grid.

In this example the small square is at (4, 2).

The *first* number, 4, is the position **left to right**.

The *second* number, 2, is the position **bottom to top**.

The position (4, 2) is where the two cross over.

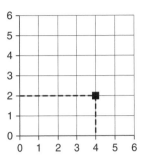

S4/4

1   Copy the grid on the right and mark on it:

    (a)   a letter **E** at (7, 3)

    (b)   a letter **I** at (4, 1)

    (c)   a letter **L** at (6, 2)

    (d)   a letter **M** at (2, 2)

    (e)   a letter **O** at (6, 2) and also at (6, 6)

    (f)   a letter **S** at (2, 3)

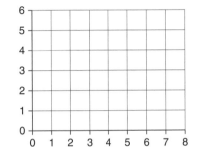

2   Write the co-ordinates for these features on the map:

    (a)   the library ....

    (b)   the school ....

    (c)   the fire station ....

    (d)   the traffic lights ....

    (e)   the supermarket ....

    (f)   the Red Lion Hotel ....

    (g)   the playing fields ....

    (h)   the Health Centre ....

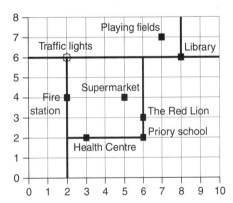

3   Add the following onto the map and mark the co-ordinates:

    (a)   swimming baths at ....   (b)   a petrol station at ....

Challenge

Draw a 10 × 10 grid and mark 5 objects on it. With a partner give co-ordinates of each other's objects to put on the other's grid.

Compare both grids to see if you are both right.

Unit M3/1 Length, mass and capacity

PNS Framework objective

- Know the relationships between kilometres and metres, metres and centimetres, kilograms and grams, litres and millilitres; choose and use appropriate units to estimate, measure and record measurements.

Unit learning outcome

- To know the relationship between metric units of length, mass and capacity.

Prior knowledge

- Understanding of the difference between length, mass and capacity.

Starter activity

- Brainstorm things that can be bought from a variety of shops and categorise them according to the way you specify how much you wish to buy – by number, mass (weight), length and volume (or capacity of the container). Point out that when buying by number, e.g. one packet of cornflakes, there can still be a second criterion, e.g. the size of the packet expressed according to the weight of the contents.

  Have a team quiz based on naming something that is sold by length, mass or volume. Use a dice to decide what is asked for each time, i.e.: 1 or 2 = sold by length, 3 or 4 = by weight, 5 or 6 = by volume.

Answers to M3/1

1 200 cm	**2** 4 m	**3** 250 cm	**4** 6 m	**5** 400 cm
6 350 cm	**7** 3 m	**8** 550 cm	**9** $3\frac{1}{2}$ m	**10** 5 cm line drawn
11 10 cm line drawn	**12** 15 cm line drawn			
13 2500 g	**14** 1 kg	**15** $3\frac{1}{2}$ kg	**16** 4000 g	**17** 500 g
18 250 g	**19** $\frac{1}{2}$ kg	**20** $2\frac{1}{2}$ kg	**21** 750 g	**22** 500 ml
23 2 l	**24** 2500 ml	**25** 3 l	**26** 4000 ml	**27** 5 l
28 1 l	**29** 250 ml	**30** 750 ml		

Unit M3/1 Length, mass and capacity

We measure length in metres (you can write just m for metres). 1 m = 100 centimetres
For shorter lengths we use centimetres (you can write just cm for centimetres).
100 cm = 1 metre

A metre is about the length of two of your strides.
A centimetre is about the width of the tip of your little finger.
Complete the conversions below.
Examples: $1\frac{1}{2}$ metres = 150 cm, 5 m = 500 cm, 8 m = 800 cm

1 2 m = ………. cm

2 ………. m = 400 cm

3 $2\frac{1}{2}$ m = ………. cm

4 ………. m = 600 cm

5 4 m = ………. cm

6 $3\frac{1}{2}$ m = ………. cm

7 ………. m = 300 cm

8 $5\frac{1}{2}$ m = ………. cm

9 ………. m = 350 cm

Draw straight lines in your book these lengths:

10 5 cm

11 10 cm

12 15 cm

We measure mass (weight) in grams (shortened to g) and kilograms (shortened to kg).
1000 grams = 1 kilogram. 'Kilo' means 1000. 1 litre of pure water weighs 1 kg.

Complete the conversions below.
Examples: $1\frac{1}{2}$ kg = 1500 g, 5 kg = 5000 g, 8 kg = 8000 g

13 $2\frac{1}{2}$ kg = ………. g

14 1000 g = ………. kg

15 3500 g = ………. kg

16 ………. g = 4 kg

17 $\frac{1}{2}$ kg = ………. g

18 $\frac{1}{4}$ kg = ………. g

19 200 g + 300 g = …. kg

20 2 kg + 500 g = …. kg

21 $\frac{3}{4}$ kg = ………. g

Capacity is a measure of the space inside a container.
A cube-shaped container measuring 10 cm tall, 10 cm wide and 10 cm deep has a capacity of 1 litre (l)
For smaller amounts we use millilitres (ml). 1 litre = 1000 ml. 1 litre of pure water weighs 1 kg.
Complete the conversions below.
Examples: $1\frac{1}{2}$ l = 1500 ml, 5 l = 5000 ml, 8 l = 8000 ml

22 $\frac{1}{2}$ l = ………. ml

23 ………. l = 2000 ml

24 $2\frac{1}{2}$ l = ………. ml

25 3000 ml = ………. l

26 4 l = ………. ml

27 ………. l = 5000 ml

28 500 ml + $\frac{1}{2}$ l = ………. l

29 $\frac{1}{4}$ l = ………. ml

30 $\frac{3}{4}$ l = ………. ml

Challenge

If 1 litre of water weighs 1 kg how many ml of water weigh 1 gram?

Mould plasticine around a cm cube to make a 1 ml measure. Put it on a set of electronic scales and see if you can weigh 1 ml of water.

Unit M3/2 Measuring with decimals

PNS Framework objective

- Know the relationships between kilometres and metres, metres and centimetres, kilograms and grams, litres and millilitres; choose and use appropriate units to estimate, measure and record measurements.

Unit learning outcome

- To use decimal notation in measures.

Prior knowledge

- Familiar with units of measure for length, mass and volume/capacity.
- Understanding of place value.

Starter activity

- Before the lesson make a large 'place value multiplier' (as illustrated).

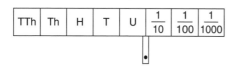

Write a three-digit number beneath the HTU columns. Remind pupils that the decimal point always comes between the units column from the tenths, separating whole numbers from 'numerals' that represent less than a whole number.

Demonstrate sliding it one, two and three columns to the left and right to divide and multiply by factors of 10, 100 and 1000. Point out the need to add in zeros between the numerals and the decimal point multiplying integers.

Go through more examples and then use it specifically to convert cm to m, m to cm, g to kg, kg to g, etc.

Answers to M3/2

1 150 cm	**2** 2 m	**3** 250 cm	**4** 3.25 m	**5** 325 cm
6 2.50 m or 2½ m	**7** 275 cm	**8** 1.85 m	**9** 721 cm	**10** 2000 g
11 1000 ml	**12** 1.5 kg	**13** 2½ or 2.00 l	**14** 2500 g	**15** 1250 ml
16 2.750 l	**17** 1.725 l	**18** 4750 g	**19** 750 ml	**20** 1750 ml
21 200 g	**22** 0.33 l	**23** 3252 g	**24** 1.245 l	**25** 11 722 g
26 1.534 kg	**27** 2.955 kg	**28** 3.525 kg	**29** 40 861 ml	**30** 0.538 l

Unit M3/2 Measuring with decimals

To change metres to cm we need to multiply by 100.

To do this move the numerals two columns to the left. You may have to put in zeros to fill the empty columns.

	H	T	U
2×100			2
	2	0	0 = 200 cm

To change centimetres into metres we divide by 100 by moving the numerals two columns to the right. Make sure there is a decimal point . to the right of the units before you start.

	H	T	U
Example: 300 cm ÷ 100 =	3	0	0.
			3.0 = 3.0 metres

Put in a decimal point if there isn't one there already. (You don't need the last 0 because there are no more numerals.)

Make the conversions below by multiplying or dividing by 100.

1	1.5 m = ... cm	2	200 cm = ... m	3	2.50 m = ... cm
4	325 cm = ... m	5	3.25 m = ... cm	6	250 cm = ... m
7	2.75 m = ... cm	8	185 cm = ... m	9	7.21 m = ... cm

When we change kg to g or l to ml we multiply by 1000. We do this by moving the numerals three columns to the left.

To change g to kg or ml to l we divide by 1000 by moving the numerals three columns to the right.

Make the conversions below by multiplying or dividing by 1000.

10	2 kg = ... g	11	1 l = ... ml	12	1500 g = ... kg
13	2500 ml = ... l	14	2.5 kg = ... g	15	1.25 l = ... ml
16	2750 g = ... kg	17	1725 ml = ... l	18	4.75 kg = ... g
19	.75 l = ... ml	20	1.75 l = ... ml	21	0.2 kg = ... g
22	330 ml = ... l	23	3.252 kg = ... g	24	1245 ml = ... l
25	11.722 kg = ... g	26	1534 g = ... kg	27	2955 g = ... kg
28	3525 g = ... kg	29	40.861 l = ... ml	30	538 ml = ... l

Challenge

Use squared paper to make a moveable label for your columns with a decimal point beneath like this:

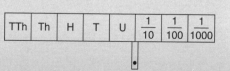

TTh	Th	H	T	U	$\frac{1}{10}$	$\frac{1}{100}$	$\frac{1}{1000}$

Place it on squared paper and write numerals beneath H, T and U. Slide it to the left and right to change the value of the numbers you have written.

Unit M3/3 Scales

PNS Framework objective

- Read, to the nearest division and half-division, scales that are numbered or partially numbered; use the information to measure and draw to a suitable degree of accuracy.

Unit learning outcome

- To read and estimate measurements from scales.

Prior knowledge

- Familiar with using rulers and tape measures for measuring in cm.
- Understand that intermediate positions between numbers also have a value.

Starter activities

- Measure the room temperature using at least one type of thermometer; if possible use a traditional alcohol thermometer and a dial one. Look at the numbering on the scale – does it go up in ones or twos?
- Measure the length of a few objects in cm, particularly things that are not an exact number of cm (e.g. compare the length of used pencils). Estimate the lengths by looking between the numbers on the scale.

Answers to M3/3

1 (a) A = 55, B = 135, C = 185, D = 165, E = 110, F = 75, G = 30, H = 205

(b) 5

2 (a) A = 250 g, B = 750 g, C = 100 g, D = 900 g, F = 450 g, G = 550 g, H = 1250 g

(b) 50 g

3 (a) A = 25 g, B = 600 g, C = 95 g, D = 130 g, E = 150 g, F = 180 g, G = 205 g, H = 225 g, I = 245 g, J = 260 g

(b) 5 g

Unit M3/3 Scales

When we measure anything properly we usually have to use a scale, either along a straight line or curved around a dial.

Sometimes what we are measuring comes between the numbers and we have to look at smaller divisions like here, the rod measures **$7\frac{1}{2}$ cm**.

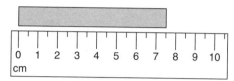

Different scales have different sized divisions. You have to look at the smaller divisions.

M3/3

1 (a) Write down the marked readings on this scale.

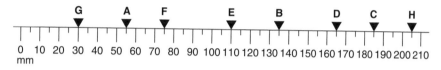

A= ...... B = ... C = ... D = ... E = ... F = ... G = ... H = ...

(b) Each of the smallest divisions on this scale represents ....

2 (a) Write down what is shown by A, B, C, D, E, F, G and H on this scale; be careful!

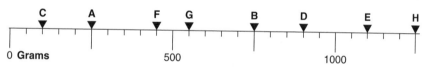

A= ...... B = ... C = ... D = ... E = ... F = ... G = ... H = ...

(b) Each of the smallest divisions on this scale represents ....

3 (a) Try this circular scale:

A= ...... B = ... C = ... D = ...
E = ... F = ... G = ... H = ...
I = ... J = ...

(b) Each of the smallest divisions on this scale represents ....

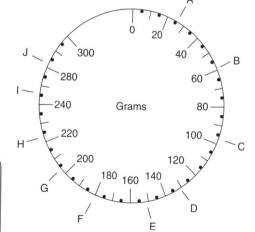

Challenge

Make a list of instruments that have a scale or dial on them.

Write down what it measures and the units it measures in (cm, kg, °C, etc.).

Unit M3/4 Reading the time

PNS Framework objective

- Read the time on a 12-hour digital clock and to the nearest five minutes on an analogue clock; calculate time intervals and find start or end times for a given time interval.

Unit learning outcome

- To read clocks to the minute and record time appropriately.

Prior knowledge

- Knows the number of minutes in an hour.
- Familiar with the terms 'digital' and 'analogue'.

Starter activities

- Ask what time pupils go to bed and write the times on the whiteboard in whatever format they say (e.g. 8:30, minutes to/past, quarter to/past). Join up times that are the same. Write times on the whiteboard and invite pupils to write the same time in a different format (e.g. write up 7:45 and get pupils to supply 'quarter to eight', 'fifteen minutes to 8').

  Collect pairs of equivalent times using minutes to and minutes past, i.e. '10 to 5' is the same as 4:50.

- Ask pupils to draw analogue and digital clocks on the whiteboard showing the same time.

Answers to M3/4

1 These times may vary in the way they are expressed
    (a) Ten o'clock   (b) A quarter past eight   (c) Ten past three
    (d) 20 to six   (e) Five to five   (f) Five past 11
    (g) 20 past nine   (h) 20 to seven   (i) Half past seven

2
       (c)   

    (a)   (b)   (c)   (d)

3 (a) Half past four   (b) Seven o'clock   (c) Five to three
    (d) Quarter to five   (e) 25 past ten   (f) 20 past one

Unit M3/4 Reading the time

We measure the passage of time during the day using clocks and watches. There are two types of display, **digital** and **analogue**.

A digital display uses changing numerals.
An analogue clock uses fingers on a dial.

Whole hours

Whole minutes past the hour

9:30

The hour hand takes an hour to move from one number to the next.

Here it is half way between 9 o'clock and 10 o'clock.

The minute hand does one complete turn every hour. It takes five minutes to go from one number to the next.

Here it is halfway around so the time is half past.

1   Copy down these digital clock displays and write the time in words next to them.
    Remember there is often more than one way to say the time.
    Example: 08:50 It is 50 minutes past eight. It is ten minutes to nine.

    (a)   10:00 ....   (b)   08:15 ....   (c)   03:10 ....
    (d)   05:40 ....   (e)   04:55 ....   (f)   11:05 ....
    (g)   09:20 ....   (h)   06:40 ....   (i)   07:30 ....

2   Draw a clock face to show each of the times in question 1 (a) to (d).

(a)

(b)

(c)

(d)

3   Read these times and write them down like you did for question 1.
    They are all before 12:00 midday.

(a) ....

(b) ....

(c) ....

(d) ....

(e) ....

(f) ....

Challenge

Write down important times for a normal day for you. Work out how long you spend sleeping, working, playing, watching TV.

Unit M4/1 Decimals in money and measures

PNS Framework objectives

- Choose and use standard metric units and their abbreviations when estimating, measuring and recording length, weight and capacity; know the meaning of 'kilo', 'centi' and 'milli' and, where appropriate, use decimal notation to record measurements (e.g. 1.3 m or 0.6 kg).
- Use decimal notation for tenths and hundredths and partition decimals; relate the notation to money and measurement; position one-place and two-place decimals on a number line.

Unit learning outcome

- To use decimal notation in money and measures.

Prior knowledge

- Firm understanding of place value including decimals.

Starter activities

- Brainstorm things that the children buy with their pocket money and the prices and get them to write them down on the whiteboard. Which ones are written in £s and which in pence? Has anyone made the 'grocer's' error of putting both £ and p symbols?
- Ask a number of children how tall they are in metric units, write them down as m and cm, only m and only cm. Re-write them in the other formats – is one format easier to record?

Answers to M4/1

1	(a) 150p	(b) £0.65	(c) 299p	(d) £1.35	(e) 625p
	(f) £2.00	(g) 437p	(h) 1270p	(i) £5.05	
2	(a) 350 cm	(b) 1.25 m	(c) 225 cm	(d) 2.55 m	(e) 578 cm
	(f) 3.6 m				
3	(a) 2500 g	(b) 2.5 kg	(c) 1850 g	(d) 0.65 kg	(e) 4600 g
	(f) 1.75 kg	(g) 3540 g	(h) 2.705 kg	(i) 525 g	
4	(a) 500 ml	(b) 1.25 l	(c) 1250 ml	(d) 0.75 ml	(e) 2500 ml
	(f) 2.15 l				

Unit M4/1 Decimals in money and measures

When we write down money we do it *either* in pence with a *p* sign, *or* in pounds with a £ sign.

We should not use both signs together.

When we write money in pounds we use a decimal point . to separate the whole pounds from the pence like these examples:

T	U	$\frac{1}{10}$	$\frac{1}{100}$		
£	3 ·	2	5	=	325 p
£	0 ·	5	5	=	55 p

1 Complete the following conversions by filling in the missing part:

(a) £1.50 = ...p (b) 65p = £.......... (c) £2.99 = ...

(d) 135p = ... (e) £6.25 = ...p (f) 200p = ...

(g) £4.37 = ... (h) £12.70 = ...p (i) 505p = ...

We can change metres into centimetres in just the same way using decimals.

2 Complete the following conversions. Examples: 1.5 m = 150 cm, 75 cm = 0.75 m

(a) 3.50 m = ... cm (b) 125 cm = ... m (c) 2.25 m = ... cm

(d) 255 cm = ... m (e) 5.78 m = ... cm (f) 360 cm = ... m

Changing kilograms into grams is similar, but remember there are 1000 grams in 1 kilogram.

3 Complete these conversions. Examples: 1.5 kg = 1500 g, 750 g = 0.75 kg

(a) 2.5 kg = ... g (b) 2500 g = ... kg (c) 1.85 kg = ... g

(d) 650 g = ... kg (e) 4.6 kg = ... g (f) 1750 g = ... kg

(g) 3.54 kg = ... g (h) 2705 g = ... kg (i) 0.525 kg = ... g

We can change litres into millilitres in just the same way using decimals.

4 Complete the following conversions. Examples: 1.5 l = 1500 ml, 750 ml = 0.75 l

(a) 0.5 l = ... ml (b) 1250 ml = ... l (c) 1.25 l = ... ml

(d) 750 ml = ... l (e) 2.5 l = ... ml (f) 2150 ml = ... l

Challenge

Use squared paper to make a place value multiplier like this one.

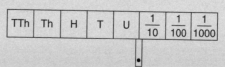

Stick it onto card and use it to make more decimal conversions.

Unit M4/2 Length, mass and capacity

PNS Framework objectives

- Choose and use standard metric units and their abbreviations when estimating, measuring and recording length, weight and capacity; know the meaning of 'kilo', 'centi' and 'milli' and, where appropriate, use decimal notation to record measurements (e.g. 1.3 m or 0.6 kg).
- Use decimal notation for tenths and hundredths and partition decimals; relate the notation to money and measurement; position one-place and two-place decimals on a number line.
- Recognise the equivalence between decimal and fraction forms of one-half, quarters, tenths and hundredths.

Unit learning outcome

- To know and use the relationships between metric units of length, mass and capacity.

Prior knowledge

- Familiar with units of measure for length, mass and volume/capacity.
- Understanding of place value.

Starter activity

- Look at the labels on a collection of (clean) food containers (jars, cans, bottles, packets) and copy the amount contained on the whiteboard, particularly including the units. Sort the amounts out according to whether they are sold by weight or volume. Sort out the packets into two sets accordingly.

  Discuss why weight is chosen for some items and volume for others. On cereal packets look for a 'contents may settle during transit' disclaimer. Discuss why some liquid items are sold by weight. Food items are not measured and sold by length – what might be sold according to length? Brainstorm items that might be bought by length.

Answers to M4/2

1	500 m	**2**	250 ml	**3**	10 cm	**4**	750 g	**5**	500 mm
6	50 cm	**7**	100 g	**8**	100 ml	**9**	100 m	**10**	25 cm
11	500 g	**12**	750 ml	**13**	1000 cm	**14**	10 000 mm	**15**	3000 g
16	2000 ml	**17**	5000 m	**18**	6 m	**19**	2 kg	**20**	5 km
21	3 l	**22**	10 m	**23**	7000 g	**24**	4 m	**25**	4500 g
26	650 cm	**27**	6500 mm	**28**	1750 ml	**29**	7500 m	**30**	8750 g

Unit M4/2 Length, mass and capacity

We can measure length in kilometres (km), metres (m), centimetres (cm) and millimetres (ml).

We can measure mass (weight) in kilograms (kg) and grams (g).

We can measure volume and capacity in litres (l) and millilitres (ml).

Reminders:
1 kilogram = 1000 grams
1 litre = 1000 millilitres
1 kilometre = 1000 metres
1 metre = 1000 millimetres
1 metre = 100 centimetres

M4/2

1 $\frac{1}{2}$ km = ...m

2 $\frac{1}{4}$ l = ...ml

3 $\frac{1}{10}$ m = ...cm

4 $\frac{3}{4}$ kg = ...g

5 $\frac{1}{2}$ m = ...mm

6 $\frac{1}{2}$ m = ...cm

7 $\frac{1}{10}$ kg = ...g

8 $\frac{1}{10}$ l = ...ml

9 $\frac{1}{10}$ km = ...m

10 $\frac{1}{4}$ m = ...cm

11 $\frac{1}{2}$ kg = ...g

12 $\frac{3}{4}$ l = ...ml

13 10 m = ...cm

14 10 m = ...mm

15 3 kg = ...g

16 2 l = ...ml

17 5 km = ...m

18 600 cm = ...m

19 2000 g = ...kg

20 5000 m = ...km

21 3000 ml = ...l

22 1000 cm = ...m

23 7 kg = ...g

24 4000 mm = ...m

25 $4\frac{1}{4}$ kg = ...g

26 $6\frac{1}{2}$ m = ...cm

27 $6\frac{1}{2}$ m = ...mm

28 $1\frac{3}{4}$ l = ...ml

29 $7\frac{1}{2}$ km = ...m

30 $8\frac{3}{4}$ kg = ...g

Challenge

Make lists of things or quantities that you could measure using:

millimetres, centimetres, metres, kilometres
grams, kilograms
millilitres, litres

Unit M4/3 Decimals in measuring

PNS Framework objective

- Recognise the equivalence between decimal and fraction forms of one-half, quarters, tenths and hundredths.

Unit learning outcome

- To use decimal notation in measures.

Prior knowledge

- Firm understanding of place value.
- Knowledge of decimal equivalents of $\frac{1}{4}$, $\frac{1}{2}$ and $\frac{3}{4}$.
- Able to multiply and divide by 10, 100, 1000 by moving numerals left or right by the appropriate number of column places.

Starter activities

- Give children several pieces of card (all the same size) to make 'snap' cards, marking them with $\frac{1}{4}$, $\frac{1}{2}$, $\frac{3}{4}$, 0.25, 0.5, and circles and squares quartered and shaded. Pool all the cards together and play fraction snap.
- Use computer software or Internet website maths games to practise matching up decimals with the equivalent common fractions.

Answers to M4/3

1	(a) 2.25 m	(b) 5.75 l	(c) 3.5 km	(d) 4.25 kg	(e) 2.5 cm
	(f) 10.75 kg				
2	(a) 3500 mm	(b) 4534 g	(c) 0.75 m	(d) 0.750 kg	(e) 1.5 km
	(f) 2500 ml	(g) 1.750 l	(h) 1750 m	(i) 2.345 m	(j) 2450 g
	(k) 5.5 cm	(l) 4400 g	(m) 4.508 m	(n) 750 ml	(o) 8050 ml
	(p) 105 mm	(q) 2.250 kg	(r) 0.5 l	(s) 2.57 km	(t) 0.075 kg
	(u) 1 125 000 g	(v) 1500 ml	(w) 835 cm	(x) 0.095 m	

Unit M4/3 Decimals in measuring

When we use decimals in measuring we need to remember that the decimal point is there to separate whole numbers (Thousands, Hundreds, Tens, Units) from numerals with a value of less than one whole unit (tenths, hundredths, thousandths, etc.)

Example:

Th	H	T	U	·	$\frac{1}{10}$	$\frac{1}{100}$	$\frac{1}{1000}$
1	3	4	5	·	7	5	0

This means 1345, and 7 tenths, 5 hundredths.

Here are the decimals for some common fractions: $\frac{1}{4}$ = 0.25, $\frac{1}{2}$ = 0.5, and $\frac{3}{4}$ = 0.75

1 Change these measures into decimals – example $1\frac{1}{2}$ kg = 1.5 kg
   (a) $2\frac{1}{4}$ m = ...   (b) $5\frac{3}{4}$ l = ...   (c) $3\frac{1}{2}$ km = ...
   (d) $4\frac{1}{4}$ kg = ...   (e) $2\frac{1}{2}$ cm = ...   (f) $10\frac{3}{4}$ kg = ...

2 You can change units of measure by multiplying or dividing by 10, 100 or 1000.
   To do this first make sure the decimal point is to the right of the units column.
   To multiply by 10, 100 or 1000 move the numerals one, two or three columns to the *left*.
   To divide by 10, 100 or 1000 move the numerals one, two or three columns to the *right*.
   You may have to add in zeros or delete zeros you don't need.
   Example: change 3.5 km to m, 3. × 1000 = 3500 m

   (a) 3.5 m = ...mm   (b) 4.534 kg = ...g   (c) 75 cm = ...m
   (d) 750 g = ...kg   (e) 1500 m = ...km   (f) 2.5 l = ...ml
   (g) 1750 ml = ...l   (h) 1.75 km = ...m   (i) 2345 mm = ...m
   (j) 2.45 kg = ...g   (k) 55 mm = ...cm   (l) 4.4 kg = ...g
   (m) 4508 mm = ...m   (n) 0.75 l = ...ml   (o) 8.05 m = ...mm
   (p) 10.5 cm = ...mm   (q) 2250 g = ...kg   (r) 500 ml = ...l
   (s) 2570 m = ...km   (t) 75 g = ...kg   (u) 1.125 kg = ...g
   (v) 1.5 l = ... ml   (w) 8.350 m = ...cm   (x) 95 mm = ...m

Challenge

How could you change:

          kilometres into millimetres?
          kilometres into centimetres?
          millimetres into kilometres?
          centimetres into kilometres?

   Try working out a few conversions of your own.

Unit M4/4 Scales

PNS Framework objective

- Interpret intervals and divisions on partially numbered scales and record readings accurately, where appropriate to the nearest tenth of a unit.

Unit learning outcome

- To record and estimate measures taken from scales.

Prior knowledge

- Able to count divisions on a scale line.
- Able to count in multiples.

Starter activities

- Brainstorm things that use scale (straight or dial) to measure or control a variable, e.g. oven temperature control, weighing scales, speedometer, heating thermostat, thermometer, ruler, volume control.
- Look at the scale markings on a conventional (i.e. glass and alcohol) room thermometer. *Is each division numbered?* (Usually no!) *Why not?* (Not enough room to write numerals of a readable size). *What does each division indicate?*

Answers to M4/4

1	(a) 620 g	(b) 250 g	(c) 480 g	(d) 930 g	(e) 210 g
	(f) 560 g	(g) 80 g	(h) 840 g	(i) 110 g	(j) 990 g
2	(a) 2.100 kg	(b) 4.850 kg	(c) 3.400 kg	(d) 1.250 kg	(e) 0.650 kg
	(f) 2.875 kg	(g) 4.225 kg	(h) 4.675 kg	(i) 3.975 kg	(j) 1.675 kg
3	(a) 80 ml	(b) 250 ml	(c) 140 ml	(d) 420 ml	(e) 170 ml
	(f) 390 ml	(g) 330 ml	(h) 280 ml	(i) 370 ml	(j) 450 ml

Unit M4/4 Scales

1   Read off the weights shown on this spring balance.
    Be careful, the scale goes from top to bottom.
    Each division (small mark) represents 20 g.
    Half a division represents 10 g.

(a) .... (b) .... (c) .... (d) ....
(e) .... (f) .... (g) .... (h) ....
(i) .... (j) ....

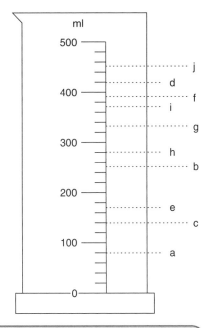

M4/4

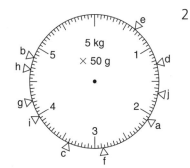

2   Read off these weights in kg.
    Each division (small mark) represents 50 g.
    Half a division represents 25 g.

(a) .... (b) .... (c) .... (d) ....
(e) .... (f) .... (g) .... (h) ....
(i) .... (j) ....

3   Read off the weights shown on this scale.
    Each division (small mark) represents 50 g.
    Half a division represents 25 g.

(a) .... (b) .... (c) .... (d)
(e) .... (f) .... (g) .... (h)
(i) .... (j) ....

Challenge

Draw new scales for the balances and measuring cylinder, using different divisions.

Can you make the scales easier to read?

Unit M4/5 Perimeters and areas

PNS Framework objective

- Draw rectangles and measure and calculate their perimeters; find the area of rectilinear shapes drawn on a square grid by counting squares.

Unit learning outcome

- To measure and calculate perimeters and area of rectangles and simple compound shapes.

Prior knowledge

- Able to add, subtract and multiply.
- Understands the term 'dimensions' and knows that flat shapes have two dimensions.

Starter activity

- Use geoboards and rubber bands to make rectangles of specified sizes.
- Race to see who can make a rectangle of specified perimeter on a geoboard first. The trick is to halve the specified perimeter and split it into two numbers.
- Race to see who can be the first to use a geoboard to make a rectangle of a specified area – avoid prime numbers!

Answers to M4/5

1. (a) P = 18 cm, area = 18 cm^2 (b) P = 22 cm, area = 24 cm^2
   (c) P = 20 cm, area = 25 cm^2 (d) P = 16 cm, area = 15 cm^2
   (e) P = 22 cm, area = 30 cm^2 (f) P = 28 cm, area = 24 cm^2
   (g) P = 20 cm, area = 21 cm^2 (h) P = 16 cm, area = 16 cm^2

2. Method 1 will vary:
   (a) 11 cm^2 (b) 18 cm^2 (c) 15 cm^2
   Method 2: (4 cm × 3 cm) – (1 cm × 1 cm)   (5 cm × 4 cm) – (2 cm × 1 cm)
   (7 cm × 3 cm) – (3 cm × 2 cm)

Unit M4/5 Perimeters and areas

The perimeter of a shape is the distance around its edges.

An easy way to find the perimeter of a rectangle is to add together its length and width then double the answer.

The area of a shape is the flat space it takes up, using its length and its width. We usually measure area in square cm (cm^2) or square metres (m^2). The ^{2} means *square* or *squared* because we are looking at two dimensions, length and width.

1   Find the perimeter and area of these rectangles:

(a) 6 cm × 3 cm
perimeter = …. cm
area = …. cm²

(b) 8 cm × 3 cm
perimeter = …. cm
area = …. cm²

(c) 5 cm × 5 cm
perimeter = …. cm
area = …. cm²

(d) 5 cm × 3 cm
perimeter = …. cm
area = …. cm²

(d) 6 cm × 5 cm
perimeter = …. cm
area = …. cm²

(e) 12 cm × 2 cm
perimeter = …. cm
area = …. cm²

(f) 7 cm × 3 cm
perimeter = …. cm
area = …. cm²

(g) 4 cm × 4 cm
perimeter = …. cm
area = …. cm²

If a shape has right angles but more than four sides like this one, we need to break it up to find the area. We can calculate the area of this shape in two different ways:

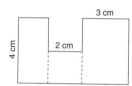

Method 1: break it into three rectangles.

(4 cm × 2 cm) + (2 cm × 2 cm) + (4 cm × 3 cm)

= 8 cm² + 4 cm² + 12 cm² = 24 cm².

Method 2: work out the area of the large rectangle and take away the area of the 'cut out'.

(4 cm × 7 cm) − (2 cm × 2 cm) = 28 cm² − 4 cm² = 24 cm².

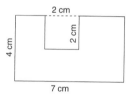

2   Use both methods to work out the area of these shapes.

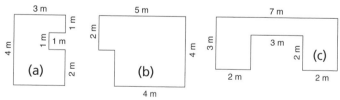

Challenge

Calculate the perimeter of these three shapes.

Draw one of your own which has the same area as one of these, but a different perimeter.

Unit M4/6 Units of time

Prior knowledge

- Knows commonly used units of time.

Starter activities

- Ask pupils to estimate the passage of one minute by closing their eyes and raising their hand and opening their eyes when they think a minute has elapsed. Count how many raise their hand in 30-second intervals. How many were close to 60 seconds?

  Discuss how activities we enjoy seem to be over quickly while less pleasant things seem to drag on. List examples of both (e.g. maths lesson, dental treatment, computer game, TV programme).

- Brainstorm examples of activities and events that might be measured using a range of units of time (having a wash, reading a book, growing 1 cm taller, going through school, etc.).

Answers to M4/6

1. (a) Second, minute, hour, day (b) Hour, day, week, year
   (c) Week, year, century, millennium
2. (a) 168 hours (b) 3600 seconds (c) 10 decades (d) 26 weeks
   (e) 260 weeks (f) 10 centuries
3. (a) 180 minutes (b) 45 years (c) 75 seconds (d) 28 days
   (e) 3 days (f) 8 weeks (g) 150 minutes (h) 336 hours
   (i) 1500 years (j) 78 weeks (k) 50 decades (l) 225 seconds
   (m) 1½ hours (n) 1½ days (o) 150 seconds (p) 105 minutes
   (q) 4 centuries (r) 3 hours (s) 500 years (t) 9 decades
   (u) 330 minutes

Unit M4/6 Units of time

When measuring time we use different sized units.

1   Arrange these units of time in ascending order, starting with the smallest.
   (a) minute, second, day, hour ....
   (b) year, day, hour, week ....
   (c) millennium, year, century, week ....
   Reminder: 1 minute = 60 seconds, 1 hour = 60 minutes, 1 day = 24 hours, week =
   7 days, 1 year = 52 weeks, 1 decade = 10 years, 1 century = 100 years, 1 millennium
   = 1000 years.

2   There are:
   (a) .... hours in 1 week   (b) .... seconds in 1 hour
   (c) .... decades in 1 century   (d) .... weeks in $\frac{1}{2}$ a year
   (e) weeks in $\frac{1}{2}$ a decade   (f) ....centuries in 1 millennium

3   Complete these time conversions:
   (a) 3 hours = ... minutes   (b) $4\frac{1}{4}$ decades = ... years
   (c) $1\frac{1}{4}$ minutes = ... seconds   (d) 4 weeks = ... days
   (e) 72 hours = ... days   (f) 56 days = ... hours
   (g) $2\frac{1}{2}$ hours = ... minutes   (h) 2 weeks = ... hours
   (i) $1\frac{1}{2}$ millennia = ... years (j) $1\frac{1}{2}$ years = ... weeks
   (k) 5 centuries = ... decades   (l) $3\frac{3}{4}$ minutes = ... seconds
   (m) 90 minutes = ... hours   (n) 36 hours = ... days
   (o) $2\frac{1}{2}$ minutes = ... seconds (p) $1\frac{3}{4}$ hours = ... minutes
   (q) 400 years = ... centuries   (r) 180 minutes = ... hours
   (s) 5 centuries = ... years   (t) 90 years = ... decades
   (u) $5\frac{1}{2}$ hours = ... minutes

Challenge

Make a list of events or happenings (for example: a TV programme, football match,
playtime, school week, school term).

Now list them in order of duration starting with the shortest.

Unit M4/7 Time intervals

PNS Framework objective

- Read time to the nearest minute; use a.m., p.m. and 12-hour clock notation; choose units of time to measure time intervals; calculate time intervals from clocks and timetables.

Unit learning outcome

- To calculate time intervals.

Prior knowledge

- Familiar with recording time in the hh:mm format.
- Can count on to 60.

Starter activities

- Work out the duration of events in the school day from the start and end times.
- Look at television programmes listings – *how long is each time slot? Discuss the schedule: do the programmes fill these slots completely? How much time is spent on commercial breaks and trailers for other programmes?*
- Look at a bus or train timetable – *do all the journeys take the same time? Are the time intervals between buses/trains the same throughout the day?*

Answers to M4/7

1
(a) 40 mins
(b) 40 mins
(c) 1 hour, 15 mins
(d) 25 mins
(e) 50 mins
(f) 55 mins
(g) 1 hour, 30 mins
(h) 2 hours, 25 mins
(i) 1 hour, 15 mins
(j) 32 mins
(k) 1 hour
(l) 1 hour, 10 mins
(m) 2 hours, 6 mins
(n) 3 hours, 25 mins
(o) 6 hours, 36 mins
(p) 59 mins
(q) 8 hours, 30 mins
(r) 5 hours, 49 mins
(s) 30 mins
(t) 3 hours, 5 mins
(u) 2 hours, 37 mins

2
(a) 35 seconds
(b) 35 seconds
(c) 2 minutes, 15 seconds
(d) 4 minutes, 50 seconds
(e) 4 minutes, 20 seconds
(f) 6 minutes, 59 seconds
(g) 11 seconds
(h) 1 minute, 29 seconds
(i) 2 minutes, 38 seconds

Unit M4/7 Time intervals

Sometimes we need to work out the interval between two times, such as how long a journey takes. An easy way to do this in your head is by counting on from the earlier time to the later one.

Example: How long from 3:25 to 5:15?

Add on **35** minutes to get from 03:25 to 04:00, add **1 hour** to get to 05:00, then add the **15 minutes** to 05:15 = *1 hour and 50 minutes*.

```
    35 mins         +  1 hour        +  15 mins      = 1 hours, 50 mins
              →   4:00        →   5:00
3:25                                                 5:15
```

Another way is to make the minutes the same like this:

```
    20 mins         +  2 hours       = 2 hours, 20 mins
              →  10:50       →
10:30                         12:50
```

1   Calculate these time intervals:
   (a) 07:10 to 07:50 ....   (b) 07:30 to 08:10 ....   (c) 04:40 to 05:55 ....
   (d) 10:55 to 11:20 ....   (e) 08:45 to 09:35 ....   (f) 11:25 to 12:20 ....
   (g) 06:25 to 07:55 ....   (h) 08:15 to 10:40 ....   (i) 09:35 to 10:50 ....
   (j) 07:21 to 07:53 ....   (k) 09:17 to 10:17 ....   (l) 10:36 to 11:46 ....
   (m) 03:38 to 05:44 ....   (n) 09:28 to 12:53 ....   (o) 05:12 to 11:48 ....
   (p) 08:54 to 09:53 ....   (q) 04:10 to 12:40 ....   (r) 05:37 to 11:26 ....
   (s) 12:50 to 13:20 ....   (t) 11:45 to 14:50 ....   (u) 10:48 to 13:25 ....

These time intervals are in minutes and seconds. We sometimes use a ' as a sign for minutes and a " as a sign for seconds; example 4' 30" means 4 minutes and 30 seconds.

2   Calculate these shorter time intervals using either of the 'counting on' methods.
   (a) 24' 20" to 24' 55" ....   (b) 36' 40" to 37' 15" ....
   (c) 53' 40" to 55' 55" ....   (d) 45' 35" to 50' 25" ....
   (e) 16' 35" to 20' 55" ....   (f) 52' 55" to 59' 54" ....
   (g) 27' 29" to 27' 40" ....   (h) 37' 43" to 39' 12" ....
   (i) 42' 48" to 45' 26" ....

Challenge

Use a stop watch to time yourself and a partner turning a book over ten times, first with your right hand and then with your left. Work out the differences in the time taken.

Can you explain the differences?

Unit D3/1 Tally charts and frequency tables

PNS Framework objective

- Answer a question by collecting, organising and interpreting data; use tally charts, frequency tables, pictograms and bar charts to represent results and illustrate observations; use ICT to create a simple bar chart.

Unit learning outcome

- To construct and interpret tally charts and frequency tables.

Prior knowledge

- Able to count in fives.

Starter activities

- Draw around hands and cut them out. Stick several cut-out hands in a row on the whiteboard and count the digits in fives. What if we added 1/2/3/4 more fingers, how many now?
- Play 'Finger Snap'.

  How to play: Two volunteers stand at the front and on the count of three they show a number between one and ten by holding up fingers/thumbs. For numbers above four they must show a complete hand of five digits. If they both show the same number it's a 'snap'. The first person to correctly call out 'snap' followed by the number of digits wins a point for their team. After a few goes change the volunteers for two pairs – one of each pair can only display no, five or ten digits each time while their partner can use any number up to ten.

Answers to D3/1

1 3 **2** 6 **3** 10 **4** 8 **5** 11 **6** 14 **7** 4 **8** 7 **9** 16 **10** 7 **11** 12 **12** 18

13 卌 II
14 卌 IIII
15 卌 I
16 卌 卌 卌
17 卌 卌 IIII
18 卌 卌 II
19 卌 卌 卌 I
20 卌 卌 卌 卌
21 卌 卌 卌 II
22 卌 卌 卌 卌 卌
23 卌 卌 卌 IIII
24 卌 卌 卌 卌 II

25

Vehicles passing school in ten minutes		
Type of vehicle	**Tally**	**Total**
Bicycles	卌 II	7
Motorbikes	III	3
Cars	卌 卌 卌 卌 III	**23**
Buses	II	2
Small vans	卌 卌 卌 IIII	19
Lorries	卌 卌 I	**11**

Unit D3/1 Tally charts and frequency tables

Tallying is a useful way of counting. It is just like counting on your fingers but you write it down.

The first four fingers are written as sticks like this: IIII

The fifth finger (your thumb) goes across to complete the handful Ɫ卄

It is easy to count in fives then add on 'loose' tally marks Ɫ卄 Ɫ卄 III 5 + 5 + 3 = 13

Write in the totals of these sets of tally marks.

1 III = ...   2 Ɫ卄 I = ...   3 Ɫ卄 Ɫ卄 = ...

4 Ɫ卄 III = ...   5 Ɫ卄 Ɫ卄 I = ...   6 Ɫ卄 Ɫ卄 IIII = ...

7 IIII = ...   8 Ɫ卄 IIII = ...   9 Ɫ卄 Ɫ卄 Ɫ卄 I = ...

10 Ɫ卄 II = ...   11 Ɫ卄 Ɫ卄 II = ...   12 Ɫ卄 Ɫ卄 Ɫ卄 I = ...

Draw tally marks for the totals given below.

13 .... = 7	14 .... = 9	15 .... = 6
16 .... = 15	17 .... = 14	18 .... = 12
19 .... = 16	20 .... = 20	21 .... = 17
22 .... = 25	23 .... = 19	24 .... = 22

25 Here are the results of a traffic survey in a *frequency table*.

Complete the missing details.

Vehicles passing school in ten minutes		
Type of vehicle	**Tally**	**Total**
Bicycles		7
Motorbikes		3
Cars	Ɫ卄 Ɫ卄 Ɫ卄 Ɫ卄 III	
Buses		2
Small vans		19
Lorries	Ɫ卄 Ɫ卄 I	

Challenge

Conduct a survey of who likes to watch what on TV.

Collect your data by tallying and total the results.

Unit D3/2 Bar charts

PNS Framework objective

- Answer a question by collecting, organising and interpreting data; use tally charts, frequency tables, pictograms and bar charts to represent results and illustrate observations; use ICT to create a simple bar chart.

Unit learning outcome

- To construct and interpret bar charts.

Prior knowledge

- Understands the principle of simple surveys and how they are conducted.
- Appropriate fine motor skills for drawing a bar chart on squared paper.

Starter activity

- Conduct a simple survey on a subject that interests the class, e.g. favourite pop star, football team, TV programme. Ask around the class using tallying on the whiteboard. Introduce the term **frequency chart** – 'frequency' means 'how often' – and make one from the tally.

  Discuss the data in the chart then draw a bar chart on the whiteboard. Point out the key features: title, scales and axis labels.

Answers to D3/2

1 (a)

Drink	Number
Chocolate	5
Coffee	3
Milk	4
Pop	8
Squash	6
Tea	2

(b) 10
(c) 18
(d) Pop, squash, hot chocolate, milk, coffee, tea

2 (a) 2 (b) 3 (c) 15 (d) 18 (e) 14 (f) Motorbike
(g) Walk, car, bus, bike, motorbike

3

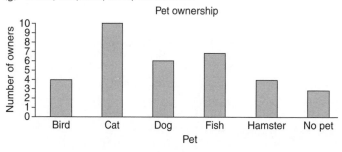

Unit D3/2 Bar charts

When we have collected data and put it into a frequency chart we can use it to make a *bar chart*. This makes it easier to compare things.

1   Here is a bar chart and its frequency table.

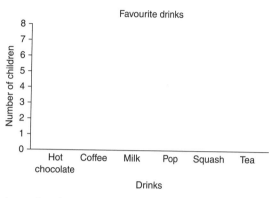

Drink	Number
Chocolate	5
Coffee	3
Milk	4
Pop	8
Squash	6
Tea	2

D3/2

(a) Use the bar chart to put the missing data into the frequency chart.

(b) How many children prefer hot drinks? ....

(c) How many children prefer cold drinks? ....

(d) List the drinks in order, starting with the most popular ....

2   Here is another bar graph.

(a) How many cycle to school? ....

(b) How many walk on their own? ....

(c) How many walk with someone else? ....

(d) How many walk altogether? ....

(e) How many travel in a vehicle? ....

(f) Which vehicle is not used? ....

(g) List the modes of transport in order, starting with the most popular. ....

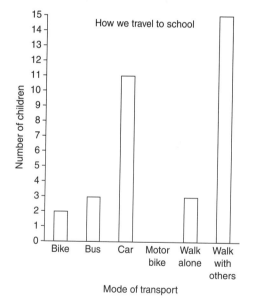

3   Use this frequency chart to draw a bar chart on squared paper.

Pet ownership	
Bird	4
Cat	10
Dog	6
Fish	7
Hamster	4
No pet	3

Challenge

Conduct a survey of your own – check your idea with your teacher first!

Collect your data and put it in a frequency chart. Draw a bar graph to show the results.

Unit D3/3 Venn diagrams

PNS Framework objective

- Use Venn diagrams or Carroll diagrams to sort data and objects using more than one criterion.

Unit learning outcome

- To construct and interpret a Venn diagram (two criteria).

Prior knowledge

- Firm grasp of what a 'set' is.

Starter activity

- Gather the children together at one end of the room and then ask all the boys to go to one area of the room and all the girls to another. Now ask them to move to another identified area according to whether they do or don't like a particular named sport, TV programme or celebrity.

  Choose new criteria, such as 'likes football' and 'likes rounders'. Identify an area of the room for each; but before asking people to move ask if anyone likes both. *Where should you people go then?* Identify an area between the other two areas. Repeat with another pair criteria that are not mutually exclusive, identifying the space between for those who belong in both groups.

Answers to D3/3

1   (a) Sarah and Jason   (b) 5   (c) 6   (d) 4   (e) 17

2

Children who like to read fiction books   Children who like to read non-fiction books

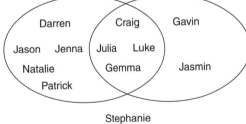

Stephanie

3   Accept any viable questions and answers about the children in the survey

---

Unit D3/3 Venn diagrams

1   Use this Venn diagram to answer these questions.

(a)   Which children don't like either swimming or football? ....

(b)   How many like swimming but not football? ....

(c)   How many like football but not swimming? ....

(d)   Which children like both? ....

(e)   How many children were in this survey? ....

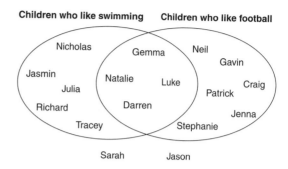

Children who like swimming   **Children who like football**

Nicholas   Gemma   Neil

Gavin

Jasmin   Natalie   Luke   Craig

Julia   Patrick

Richard   Darren

Jenna

Tracey   Stephanie

Sarah   Jason

2   Use this information to fill in this Venn diagram about reading.

Darren likes football stories.
Gavin likes books about history.
Jasmin likes cookery books.
Natalie likes Roald Dahl's stories.
Stephanie doesn't like any books!
Jenna likes horror stories.
Craig likes any book about pirates.
Jason likes stories about cowboys.
Julia reads stories and non-fiction about football.
Luke reads any book about fishing.
Patrick reads Harry Potter books.
Gemma reads stories and books about wildlife.

Children who like to read fiction books   **Children who like to read non-fiction books**

3   Make up five questions and answers that you could ask about the children in this Venn diagram.

Question   Answer

....

....

....

....

....

Challenge

Conduct a survey of your own, asking people about two things. Draw and label a Venn diagram first, then write names in the correct places when you ask people.

Unit D3/4 Carroll diagrams

PNS Framework objective

- Use Venn diagrams or Carroll diagrams to sort data and objects using more than one criterion.

Unit learning outcome

- To construct and interpret a Carroll diagram (two criteria).

Prior knowledge

- Firm grasp of what a 'set' is.

Starter activities

- Divide the room in half lengthways and ask all the boys to stand in one half and all the girls in the other. Place labels on the end walls to identify the two halves as 'boys' and 'girls'. Now divide the room in half widthways, and specify that everyone born in the first half of the year must stand on one side of the division and those born July to December on the other side. Place labels on the side walls. Check that none of the children have migrated over to the other gender's half of the room. Discuss the properties of the group standing in each quarter of the room (boys January to June, boys July to December, girls January to June, girls July to December).
- Choose new criteria such as 'eats school dinners' and 'does not eat school dinners' and label the walls accordingly. Confirm the properties of each group. Repeat with another pair criteria of mutually exclusive criteria.

Answers to D3/4

1 (a) 9   (b) Natalie and Sarah   (c) 6   (d) 5
(e) Julia, Tracey, Patrick and Stephanie

2

	Can swim	Can't swim
Boys	Ashley Richard Lee Ryan Jake Darren	Gholam Ivan Patrick Liam Tyler
Girls	Leanne Danielle Kristy Lindsey Rachel	Gemma Sarah Amy Tracey

3 Accept any viable questions and answers about the children in the survey.

Unit D3/4 Carroll diagrams

This is called a Carroll diagram. It is another way of giving information that has been sorted.

Children were asked if they liked playing football and rounders. Their names were put on the diagram.

	Like rounders	Don't like rounders
Like football	Luke Gemma Jason Craig Ashley	Gavin Darren Kristy Richard
Don't like football	Julia Tracey Patrick Stephanie	Natalie Sarah

The row shows if they like football and the column shows if they like rounders.

1   Use the Carroll diagram to find the answers to these questions.

(a)   How many of the children like playing football? ....

(b)   Which children don't like playing either football or rounders? ....

(c)   How many children don't like playing rounders? ....

(d)   How many like playing both football and rounders? ....

(e)   Which children like rounders but not football? ....

2   A teacher needs to sort boys and girls who can or can't swim. Those who can swim have a letter S by their name.

Boys
S Ashley, Gholam, S Richard, S Lee, Ivan, Patrick, S Ryan, Liam, S Jake, S Darren, Tyler

Girls
Gemma, S Leanne, Sarah, S Danielle, S Kristy, S Lindsey, Amy, Tracey, S Rachel

	Can swim	Can't swim
Boys		
Girls		

3   Make up three questions and answers that you could ask about this Carroll diagram.

Question	Answer
....	....
....	....
....	....

Challenge

Make up a Carroll diagram of your own that you can make without asking anyone questions. For example, *hot/cold* and *food/drink*.

Unit D4/1 Tally and frequency charts

PNS Framework objective

- Answer a question by identifying what data to collect; organise, present, analyse and interpret the data in tables, diagrams, tally charts, pictograms and bar charts, using ICT where appropriate.

Unit learning outcome

- To construct and interpret tally charts and frequency tables.

Prior knowledge

- Able to count multiples of 5 and quickly add on 1, 2, 3 or 4.

Starter activities

- Practise tallying with familiar tally marks then try other methods.

    | || ||| |||| LHH

    | ⌐   ⊓   ☐   ☒

- Conduct a simple survey (e.g. favourite TV programme) and ask children to come out to the whiteboard in turn and put their tally mark in the right place to show their preference.

    Try a second survey, but this time using 'like' instead of 'favourite', thus allowing children to add a tally mark to more than one option. Total up to find which is the most popular.

Answers to D4/1

1   (a) 7   (b) 11   (c) 8   (d) 14   (e) 19   (f) 21   (g) 16   (h) 24   (i) 17   (j) 9

2

aeroplane	13
bus	24
car	26
ferry	7
hovercraft	2
train	11

3   Car, bus, aeroplane, train, ferry, hovercraft

Unit D4/1 Tally and frequency charts

Tallying is a useful way of counting. It is just like counting on your fingers but you write it down.

The first four fingers are written as sticks like this: ||||

The fifth finger (your thumb) goes across to complete the handful ⌊⌿⌿⌉

It is easy to count in fives then add on 'loose' tally marks. ⌊⌿⌿⌉ ⌊⌿⌿⌉ ||| 5 + 5 + 3 = 13

1   Count up these tallies.

(a) ⌊⌿⌿⌉ || = ...

(b) ⌊⌿⌿⌉ ⌊⌿⌿⌉ | = ...

(c) ⌊⌿⌿⌉ ||| = ...

(d) ⌊⌿⌿⌉ ⌊⌿⌿⌉ |||| = ...

(e) ⌊⌿⌿⌉ ⌊⌿⌿⌉ ⌊⌿⌿⌉ |||| = ...

(f) ⌊⌿⌿⌉ ⌊⌿⌿⌉ ⌊⌿⌿⌉ ⌊⌿⌿⌉ | = ...

(g) ⌊⌿⌿⌉ ⌊⌿⌿⌉ ⌊⌿⌿⌉ | = ...

(h) ⌊⌿⌿⌉ ⌊⌿⌿⌉ ⌊⌿⌿⌉ ⌊⌿⌿⌉ |||| = ...

(i) ⌊⌿⌿⌉ ⌊⌿⌿⌉ ⌊⌿⌿⌉ || = ...

(j) ⌊⌿⌿⌉ |||| = ...

When we use these marks in a table like this we call it a *tally chart*.

2   Complete the tally chart by filling in the numbers.

3   List the modes of transport in order starting with the highest frequency.

....

....

....

How many people have travelled by:

Aeroplane	⌊⌿⌿⌉ ⌊⌿⌿⌉ |||	
Bus	⌊⌿⌿⌉ ⌊⌿⌿⌉ ⌊⌿⌿⌉ ⌊⌿⌿⌉ ||||	
Car	⌊⌿⌿⌉ ⌊⌿⌿⌉ ⌊⌿⌿⌉ ⌊⌿⌿⌉ ⌊⌿⌿⌉ ⌊⌿⌿⌉		
Coach	⌊⌿⌿⌉ ⌊⌿⌿⌉ ⌊⌿⌿⌉ ⌊⌿⌿⌉ ||	
Ferry	⌊⌿⌿⌉ ||	
Hovercraft	||	
Train	⌊⌿⌿⌉ ⌊⌿⌿⌉		

Challenge

Conduct a simple survey of your own. Your survey may be very simple such as a list of TV programmes that people like. If you use 'like' instead of 'favourite', people in your survey can vote for more than one! Collect the data by tallying. Put the totals into a frequency table.

Unit D4/2 Bar graphs and pictographs

PNS Framework objective

- Answer a question by identifying what data to collect; organise, present, analyse and interpret the data in tables, diagrams, tally charts, pictograms and bar charts, using ICT where appropriate.

Unit learning outcome

- To construct and interpret bar graph and pictograph.

Prior knowledge

- Understands that data can be collected and displayed in graphical form.

Starter activities

- Ask everyone to make a cut-out drawing of him/herself (give them pre-cut paper and specify head at the top edge and feet at the bottom edge). Use them to make a simple pictograph on the whiteboard (e.g. shoe size), each child sticking their cut-out in the appropriate row. Try another pictograph survey.
- Use the same data to draw a bar chart on the whiteboard.
- Before starting question 2, demonstrate how to estimate where the tops of some of the bars should be.

Answers to D4/2

1. (a) Reception: 18   Class 1: 15   Class 2: 11   Class 3: 14
       Class 4: 8   Class 5: 12   Class 6: 19
   (b) Total: 97
   (c) Class 6, Reception, Class 1, Class 3, Class 5, Class 2, Class 4
   (d) 44   (e) 53   (f) 9

2. (a)

   (b) Class 4, Class 2, Class 3, Class 5, Class 1, Class 6, Reception
   (c) Reception: 90   Class 1: 75   Class 2: 55   Class 3: 70   Class 4: 40   Class 5: 60
       Class 6: 95

Unit D4/2 Bar graphs and pictographs

1 Here is a **pictograph** that shows how many house points were given on one day in a school. Each whole face represents two children, a half face represents one child.

(a) How many house points did each class get on Monday?
Reception .... Class 1 ....
Class 2 ....   Class 3 ....
Class 4 ....   Class 5 ....
Class 6 ....

(b) What was the total for the day?

....

(c) List the classes in descending order, starting with the class with the highest score.

....

House points earned on monday	
Reception	☺☺☺☺☺☺☺☺☺
Class 1	☺☺☺☺☺☺☺☾
Class 2	☺☺☺☺☺☾
Class 3	☺☺☺☺☺☺☺
Class 4	☺☺☺☺
Class 5	☺☺☺☺☺
Class 6	☺☺☺☺☺☺☺☺☺☾
Key: ☺ represents two children	

(d) How many house points did each Key Stage 1 (Reception and Classes 1 and 2) get? ....

(e) How many house points did each Key Stage 2 (Classes 3 to 6) get? ....

(f) What is the difference between the Key Stage 1 and Key Stage 2 totals? ....

2 Here are the totals for the week:

Class	Rec	1	2	3	4	5	6
Total	50	45	30	36	24	43	49

(a) Complete the bar graph which has been started off.
The number scale goes up in fives so you need to estimate.
33 is slightly more than half-way between 30 and 35
32 is slightly less than half-way between 30 and 35
21 is slightly more than 20
19 is slightly less than 20

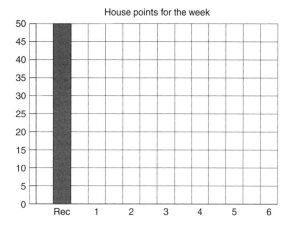

House points for the week

Challenge

Draw a bar chart to show your answer to question 2, part (c).

Unit D4/3 Venn diagrams

PNS Framework objective

- Answer a question by identifying what data to collect; organise, present, analyse and interpret the data in tables, diagrams, tally charts, pictograms and bar charts, using ICT where appropriate.

Unit learning outcome

- To construct and interpret Venn diagrams (three criteria).

Prior knowledge

- Firm grasp of what a 'set' is.
- Can understand the properties of sectors where sets overlap.

Starter activity

- Play 'human Venn diagrams' – chalk out intersecting Venn rings on the playground (not too big or the labels won't be close enough to view at the same time). Take out pre-drawn sets of labels for the rings plus 1 kg masses to weigh them down. Use one set of labels and challenge the children to find their own sector. Check that children in each sector are in the right place. Anyone found in the wrong sector is eliminated from the game and then assumes the role of assistant and extra judge.

Answers to D4/3

1. (a) All 8 sectors, including the 'universal set', each a different colour
   (b) Colours transferred to the key and appropriate descriptions similar to:
       Can swim, can't roller skate or play instrument
   (c) Philip and John can't swim
   (d) Ibrahim can't roller skate
   (e) Richard can't swim, roller skate or play an instrument

2.

Unit D4/3 Venn diagrams

1   (a)   Use different colours to crayon the eight sectors of this Venn diagram.
Use the colours in this key and describe the members of each sector.
The first one is done for you.

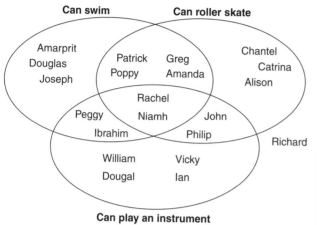

Can swim, can't roller skate or play instrument

(b)   What can't Philip and John do? ....

(c)   What can't Ibrahim do? ....

(d)   What can't Richard do? ....

2   Use the data in the table at the bottom of the sheet to complete this Venn diagram.

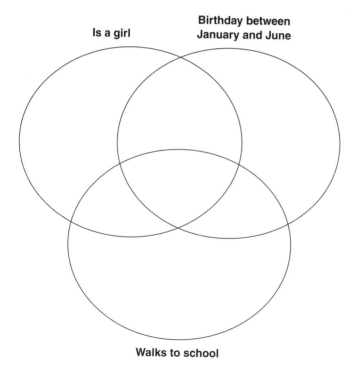

Girls	Birthday	Travel
Amanda	April	Mum drives her
Amarprit	February	Walks with sister
Catrina	August	Walks with friends
Chantel	March	Comes by bus
Niamh	December	Mum drives her
Peggy	February	Comes by bus
Poppy	October	Walks with Mum
Rachel	May	Driven by Dad
Alison	January	Walks on her own
Vicky	September	Walks with Mum

Boys	Birthday	Travel
Dougal	July	Driven by Mum
Douglas	April	Walks with friends
Greg	January	Driven by Mum
Ian	May	Walks with friends
Ibrahim	May	Driven by Mum
John	September	Walks on his own
Joseph	March	Rides a bike
Patrick	January	Walks with brothers
Philip	April	Rides a bike
Richard	June	Walks on his own
William	December	Walks with friends

Challenge

Make a Venn diagram of your own class.